MW01119883

TRUE
IDENTITY

ONE WOMAN'S JOURNEY TO JOY

IMANI N. **DODLEY-OLEAR**

BALBOA.
PRESS

A DIVISION OF HAY HOUSE

This book is a work of non-fiction. Unless otherwise noted, the author and the publisher make no explicit guarantees as to the accuracy of the information contained in this book and in some cases, names of people and places have been altered to protect their privacy.

Scripture quotations are from New Revised Standard Version Bible, copyright © 1989 National Council of the Churches of Christ in the United States of America. Used by permission. All rights reserved.

Balboa Press books may be ordered through booksellers or by contacting:

Balboa Press
A Division of Hay House
1663 Liberty Drive
Bloomington, IN 47403
www.balboapress.com
1 (877) 407-4847

Because of the dynamic nature of the Internet, any web addresses or links contained in this book may have changed since publication and may no longer be valid. The views expressed in this work are solely those of the author and do not necessarily reflect the views of the publisher, and the publisher hereby disclaims any responsibility for them.

The author of this book does not dispense medical advice or prescribe the use of any technique as a form of treatment for physical, emotional, or medical problems without the advice of a physician, either directly or indirectly. The intent of the author is only to offer information of a general nature to help you in your quest for emotional and spiritual well-being. In the event you use any of the information in this book for yourself, which is your constitutional right, the author and the publisher assume no responsibility for your actions.

Any people depicted in stock imagery provided by Thinkstock are models, and such images are being used for illustrative purposes only. Certain stock imagery © Thinkstock.

Print information available on the last page.

ISBN: 978-1-5043-9706-3 (sc)
ISBN: 978-1-5043-9707-0 (e)

Balboa Press rev. date: 01/30/2018

FOREWORD

*"The holiest of all the spots on earth is where an
ancient hatred has become a present love."*

A Course in Miracles - T-26.IX.6

L OVE IS WHAT WE ARE designed for. Love is what we are called
to give. Love is what we are to receive. Love just is. That isn't
an earth shattering message but it is life changing when we realize
and truly understand the simple truth. Love just is.

That simple truth hit me during meditation while Eric, a
man that I have been learning how to love, is away. During this
time, I started asking God, the universe, and my true self about
this concept of love. As I did, I began to feel this radiating love
I have for Eric and in that instance, I realized this type of love
isn't special because it's not just something for Eric and I. It is
something for everyone. Love just is.

The other thing that began to unpack for me is in order to
see that truth about love we have to remove the many of layers
of unforgiveness. We all have areas of forgiveness to address,
whether it's of others, or ourselves. Many times, because of our
attachments to those feelings, of lack and judgment, we forget that
forgiveness can create blinders to how we are experiencing each
other, and reacting to something within ourselves.

I have always been fascinated with the idea of forgiveness and
our resistance to it. I gravitated to truths shared by Patanjali, Mark
Twain, Dr. Ken Wapnick and even Helen Shucman, the author of
A Course in Miracles or ACIM and The Holy Bible. Forgiveness
offers us the opportunity to transform and find the love that is

accessible for all of us. This is not something that is accessible for just me but for the collective me's of the world. My hope is through the retelling of my story with Eric it will help unfold this truth. So this is a story of us… not only Eric and I, but all of us, through my eyes of how I began the practice of forgiveness in order to see love. Hopefully it will lead us to realize the truth that "*Nothing real can be threatened. Nothing unreal exists. Herein lies the peace of God.*"

FROM THE INTRODUCTION TO A COURSE IN MIRACLES:

This is a course in miracles. It is a required course. Only the time you take it is voluntary. Free will does not mean that you can establish the curriculum. It means only that you can elect what you want to take at a given time. The course does not aim at teaching the meaning of love, for that is beyond what can be taught. It does aim, however, at removing the blocks to the awareness of love's presence, which is your natural inheritance. The opposite of love is fear, but what is all-encompassing can have no opposite. This course can therefore be summed up very simply in this way:
Nothing real can be threatened.
Nothing unreal exists.
Herein lies the peace of God.

A S YOU READ EACH SECTION, I invite you to take time to pray, meditate, sit quietly, and contemplate, whatever you wish to call it but the only thing I invite you to NOT do, is hold judgment on yourself. Personally, I practice Metta Meditation. It is a form of meditation that I do on a daily basis because it has helped me to be more grounded and intentional with how I send love and light to others.

Aldous Huxley said, *"Its a bit embarrassing to have been concerned with the human problem all one's life and find at the end that one has no more to offer (by way of advice) than this: Try to be a little kinder."*

I started a practice of Metta Meditation after I encountered what someone had written in the concrete while walking in Phoenix Arizona. It said, "May All Beings Be Enlightened."

I remember stopping and looking down at the ground and chuckling to myself saying, "yea right!" And within moments then saying, "I know some pretty jerky $%^#& and there is no way they are ever going to be enlightened!" Within moments, what seemed to be the universe tapped me and saying, *"how arrogant of you daughter, these souls all have the same potential of you, how about you send some love to these so called jerks."* That was my first step to researching how I can be a little kinder and a little more loving. However, I had no idea where this journey was going to lead me.

The word, Metta, or Maitri in Sanskrit, basically means warm hearted well-wishing. It is most commonly translated as "loving-kindness" and it has been translated in the English to words such as, goodwill, benevolence, kindness, and friendliness. The loving part has a beautiful emphasis on how we can allow a flow of deep of happiness toward ourselves and others. Whereas, the kindness part suggests the love is concerned with the welfare of others. Loving-kindness meditation consists primarily of connecting to the intention of wishing happiness, wellness, safety, and peacefulness to ourselves and others.

The mantra goes like this:
May I be happy
May I be well
May I be safe
May I be peaceful

Then for others just change the personal pronoun to You and envision the person that you wish to send loving-kindness:
May YOU be happy
May YOU be well
May YOU be safe
May YOU be peaceful

So, Metta inspired me and I started by sending Metta to myself so I could begin a healing process of negative thoughts that I sent to myself, sometimes, on a daily basis. From body image issues, things I've done or not done in my past, or even for the thought of not believing everyone can be enlightened. Then something happened, the seed that I had planted in love began to grow and I started noticing that I wasn't beating myself up any longer, or at least not as much!

From there I was inspired again and I began to feel more confident in this process. I started to send out feelings of loving-kindness to people I love, people I know, like the coffee shop girl that always made my latte perfect, and yes even those I called jerks! It has been a beautiful journey. It has been revolutionary. It has been a journey of love. In the midst of this I've realized that the change may not have been in the world, but in me. I started seeing myself and others with the eyes of the universe. With eyes of love.

Do I think Metta meditation is a magic pill and everything will be perfect? No. But I do believe it starts a revolution within, because it is our true identity as humans to be people of love, forgiveness, and compassion. So I practice Metta Meditation on my cushion, mat, and in my daily walk so that I can live life inspired; so I can live a life of revolution. It's a funny thing about the word revolution - love is trapped right in the middle - look closely... rEVOLution. Love truly changes the world and it starts with us. Then maybe, 'all beings will be enlightened.'

This book is dedicated to that simple truth -
nothing real can be threatened.
This book is dedicated to God, The Divine, The
Universe and the Angels who continue to guide.
This book is dedicated to Eric, my soul mate, soul guide and soul love.
This book is dedicated to my children Hakeem and Maisha,
my forgiveness teachers.
This book is dedicated to my mother,
who still teaches me about compassion from beyond.
This book is dedicated to my father, who
helped me to stand in my truth.
This book is dedicated to all of us, trying to figure out this journey,
this time around.

CONTENTS

"The whole is greater than the sum of it's parts." Aristotle

Part 1

Part 2

Part 3

Part 4

Part 5

Part 6

Part 1

IDENTITY CRISIS

THERE HAVE BEEN TIMES IN my life I have not known who I was. I know that sounds ridiculous in many ways but it's true. I have tried to "be" whoever it was I needed to be in the midst of the situations I found myself. Whenever I dated someone, I would become whoever I needed to be to "fit" into the relationship. If it was a boyfriend that needed me to be "extra sexy" or "submissive" I tried to wear it like an bad fitting coat. At times it would become the ridiculous, like buying a set of golf clubs, taking lessons and hating every swing of the club so that I would be adored as the perfect girlfriend. However, it did not just manifest in my dating life, it was a theme that hit every area, whether it was with family, ways of community service, my jobs, wherever! I was a chameleon and not having any idea of how to walk in my true self because I was afraid my true self was not enough.

This may have all started when I was a little girl growing up on Rich Street in Columbus Ohio. I loved my neighborhood, my friends and my "spare parts" family. These "spare parts" that are my family, included anything from new found aunts and uncles that just always were around but no blood relation at all. We had reunions and at different times all lived in one household or another together because that's what you did.

It seemed to be heaven on earth until my grandmother died. I was eleven years old and remember the day as if it was yesterday.

My grandfather was cooking liver for breakfast, as my brother and I sat on the gold tapestry couch. I wore my grandmothers robe and was coloring, and my brother Mark had his electric football

3

game running loudly. I was instructed to go upstairs to wake my grandmother up. As I walked up the 17 steps to the door of my grandparents bedroom, I hoped up on the bed in an attempt to startle my grandmother, nothing. I remember repeating, "grandma, wake up! Grandpa says its time for breakfast." Nothing. Those words seemed to echo like I was screaming into a tunnel. I saw her mouth part and she released a gentle exhale. Then nothing. In that moment I felt like love escaped.

Afterwards I went downstairs, sat back on the couch perfectly still until my grandfather came in and said, "did you go up and wake your grandmother?" I simply said, "I tried." In response, he mumbled, "she's just messing with you" and proceeded up the stairs. Afterwards all I heard was utter chaos of screams of despair from our home, while the blare of sirens became an eerie cry. As I sat there, I remember removing my grandmothers robe I had been playing in without a sound, without any additional movement and I felt my heart break. In that moment I realized, that loving someone fully would result in this feeling and I never wanted to experience that again.

There was a change in the house after my grandmother died. My father was there more frequently, as he worked on his doctorate. My grandfather was struggling with gangrene, which caused his leg to be amputated and my brother Mark was incredibly over protective of me. My "spare part" aunties, which happened to be women that was not biologically related, but gave me wisdom, advice or just plain "don't do that" lectures. I guess because I was the last girl in the house they seemed to want to make sure nothing would happen to me. However, the most conflicting advice always came from the men in the house. Their wisdom from a male perspective was riddled with fear and manipulation but they did teach me all things football, and that was at least good until this day.

Because my household was full of testosterone it seemed to be only natural that it even filled my playmates during this time. In those days of running in streets, playing tag, or hide and seek until the street lights came on, most of my friends where boys because that is what the neighborhood was mostly made of! From Bobby, Roosevelt, Bo, Chris, Brian, and others we just all hung out! As for the girls I was friends with, we just took all of this as normal and so many times a game of tag turned into football or the gentle game of rock fight! Yes, we threw literal rocks at each other trying to dodge them! I was a bit of a tomboy so hanging out with the guys was just normal for me, but I still liked getting my hair done weekly! I was a cute tomboy, and that caused a bit of stir with the boys as their testosterone turned to hormones, neither of which I paid attention to, but obviously my father did. As me and the boys sat on the stoop of my porch, after chasing down the ice cream man and just laughed about nothing, my father comes home and proceeds to scream at me for hanging so freely with the guys. I didn't get why because that's what I had always done. Before my breast had budded, thats what I did. Before I got my menses, thats what I did. However now, because of the threat of pregnancy looming, and the boys hot like a dog smelling out a his prey, my father launched into me because I guess it was easier than thinking of the possibility that one of these boys will try to knock up his daughter. So that day, for the first time, I heard my father differently. I was shocked, hurt, and a little more love left me in that moment. And all I wanted to do from that moment was please my father.

So, that meant, if it was my father who needed me to agree with something, I did so because of the desire to be who he thought I should be. However, without knowing that consciously, I began to slowly cover up my likes, dislikes, and ideas to become someone else he would love and ultimately whoever I encountered. This continued throughout my adult life, when I was in relationship with a man. If I needed to be docile because he was threatened by my opinion, I suddenly would not vocalize it. If I needed to become a temptress then I would pull out my high heels even if my feet ached in pain. So whether it was a man, or over the past few years, a congregation that I was serving as pastor, I would attempt to fit their mold. The church however, is an interesting place to adapt. My outward mantra to people who came into our doors was, "all are welcome, just as you are." However, covering up my desire for more contemplative prayer in worship or a raise of the hand in testimony or the more carnal way that I attempted to fulfill an idea is simply my desires of a healthy sexual fulfillment. All in the idea of not truly understanding my identity.

I also think I tried to convince myself I was something at times when I didn't even believe it. In my mind, I now realize that I was trying to fit in to certain status quo or whatever I had interpreted that the media, or the world said "I" was supposed to be, based on my experiences in this life. Whether it was, I should be a "victim" or even "unforgiving" because I had experienced so many different hardships in my life, I realized that none of those things determined my "story" or what my true identity rested in. It was like there was a holy whispering happening in my ears whenever I would try to play certain roles. Many times, over my life, I remember it was like I had replaced the tape that was truly in me and I seemed to attack my own truest self and in essence attacking my Creator. I knew that forgiveness was a part of me in the deepest sense and that I would be happy functioning that way. But everything around me shouted, "Don't remember!" Which reminds me of scripture that says, "19 And by this we will know that we are from the truth and will reassure our hearts before him 20 whenever our hearts condemn us; for God is greater than our hearts, and he knows everything." 1 John 3:19-20.

For me, I realized that forgiveness was the only identity I could hold onto, because if I didn't forgive the countless mundane moments or the deep rooted fears that had been created in me, then I could never be who I was called and designed to be. I realized there is something forgiveness does to a person. It helps you to see who and what your identity really is and that can move us to see even one step further, who others truly are. We often think forgiveness is about freeing ourselves from the ties that bind us and yes, there is truth to that, but it's so much more. Our identity and function in this lifetime is to begin to walk the road that is least traveled through a footpath of forgiveness so we can be moved to love. That is the fulfilling function. That is the person I needed to become. That was the person that could walk a little lighter and fuller at the same time. Lighter from hatred and fuller with love.

You want to know the secret to happiness. Forgive. You want to know why you are here on this planet. Forgive. You want to know what God wants of you. Forgive. The answer to all of life is wrapped up in those 7 letters. Forgive. Forgive. Forgive.

Forgiveness for us involves both the head and the heart, and may be one of the reasons we find it so difficult. I know I believed if I make a choice to truly turn away from all the feelings of resentment, or hurt, that I have experienced I wondered who the hell would I be. Resentment has fueled some wonderful images of inflicting hurt on someone who has hurt me. But once I began to truly see that person or the issue as just an extension of what I was wrestling with internally, I began to be more compassionate towards them and maybe even towards myself.

In the midst of loosing myself in others, I also started to fill my life with things that were not meaningful so I didn't have to be accountable to something or the some one that was calling me into a better way of being. We all try to fill in the void we have with things that don't ultimately matter. Sex, did that. Drugs, did that. Mixing the two, did that. Each act was equally unfulfilling because it was never me. It never felt good in my skin. Why is that the case? Not only for me but for all of us. Because we are uncomfortable with the true identity of ourselves, our brothers and sisters, and even those folks we don't consider tolerable and it becomes a disease. And much like a disease consumes and attacks our bodies, so the same can be said for dis-ease. Because we have forgotten to see who we are.

In an issue of TIME magazine entitled *"Why Forgive? The Pope Pardons The Gunman."* Asked in 1954 the sensual and provocative question, that is still relative for today.

Why forgive?

For many of us, if we are open to forgiveness we may still question how could anyone forgive someone who tried to take your life. But we would place heavy over tones of religiosity on it and then just settle with the answer, "oh well, it's the pope!"

However, the truth is we as individuals need to learn how to forgive because it will allow us to be free from the things of the past that keeps us imprisoned. Those bars that we stay behind because of an old grievance, keeps us trapped and unable to move forward to a new life. And as the article says,

'Not to forgive is to yield oneself to another control. If one doesn't not forgive, then one is controlled by the other's initiatives and is locked into a sequence of act and response, of outrage and revenge, tit for tat, escalating always.'

Here is my truth... my ego love tit for tat! Why? Because it allows me to think that I am to be separate from another human being. My ego tells me that I am better than another human being, because of certain circumstances and loves to compare myself to another. Furthermore, my ego definitely loves the idea of getting even with others no matter what they have done. Because, in feeling like I am separate and rolling in my own victim persona I also forget what and who we are truly created to be. Creators of forgiveness, love and compassion.

In relationships with others it is inevitable that we will be hurt, maybe over and over again. Relationships are messy, whether its a relationship with the coffee barista or with your spouse. Not only do we hurt those outside of ourselves we also hurt our inner selves with the constant chatter of comparison and judgment. We don't forgive ourselves so often and blame ourselves as if we are the root of the trouble, when Rumi would point to the simple truth that we are the cure and key to open the truth that is locked within us. We hold the truth of our own healing within but it just happens to be locked away. Maybe that is the place to start so we can offer that same forgiveness to others. Our own inner selves.

Whether we admit it or not, each of us has said or done something that has created feelings of guilt, shame, and unforgiveness. These are universal feelings. When this happens, it is like we are reliving the archetypes, Adam and Eves story, again and again by covering our shame with ego driven banters, and at times violence whether physical or mental, instead of releasing that shame and practicing forgiveness. This release, is the only way to find our true identity.

If we truly understood that each of us are made in the image of God, we would have to ask ourselves, what are we reflecting or showing in this world to others? Quite honestly I've been asking myself that very question around what madness am I perpetrating? Do I really believe that I am always in the presence of something greater or even that I am something greater because I am a reflection of God?

There is a hymn that starts of with the words, "Take my life that I may be, consecrated Lord to thee. Take my action and my thoughts…" and I didn't really understand those words until recently. I began to ask myself, "Am I open to allow God, the universe, my higher power, to lead my life and be consecrated to something bigger than me and truly manifest the image of my true identity; with my actions and my thoughts?"

Yes I am a pastor. Yes I am a yogi. And everything in between. But mostly and I think more importantly I am a soul of love that is serious about finding the truth of my true identity about that truth. I am a soul of love. A soul that should offer love to self and others. A soul that receives love. A soul that gives love.

SWEET SMELL OF FORGIVENESS

T HERE HAVE BEEN SEVERAL DEFINITIONS offered for forgiveness. They have been based on philosophy, traditional religions, psychology and even on developmental principles. Forgiveness has been labeled as condemning, seeking justice, excusing, condoning, and just plain forgetting. Forgiveness is not any of those things, as I understand it now. But rather forgiveness is generous, freeing, merciful, letting go, acceptance, and even grace.

I have in some form or another been fascinated by the area of forgiveness since my twenties. I knew that I wanted it in my life because I could feel the things I was wrestling with, even if I was unsure of the "what it was." I knew how it was affecting my life, it shut me down and off from building healthy relationships with others and mostly with who I was called to be, who I truly was. I knew I wanted to see that truth of self to manifest in people, because I knew how its absence in my own life, and those feelings of loneliness and shame could also be affecting their lives. I was apprehensive about it because whether it was forgiving myself or forgiving another person I wondered, "who would I be if I didn't hold onto this *offense?*"

So for years within my ministry I talked about, researched, lead workshops, and gave examples of forgiveness in my life but I can now see I never truly practiced it. Within Patanjali's Yoga Sutras, he writes, '*When disturbed by negative thoughts, think of their polar opposite.*[1]' I also have a mantra that I found somewhere that I use in meditation that says, '*whatever you meet in opposition*

---

[1] Sutra 2.33

today, meet with meditation.' I read both of these prior to going to a yoga class here in town and wouldn't you know it, the universe, who obviously thinks I need some guidance on the issue, had the practice be focused on forgiveness of self or another.

There was a lot of forward folds and surrendering poses, all that invites the one practicing their yoga to symbolically let go. After I completed a yoga practice, feeling little shifts in my body and heart, I began reflecting as I drove home about those areas that I keep meeting with opposition. And like a light bulb switching on in a dark room, I began to see a little more clearly. I had still not done the work of looking honestly at who hurt me, uncovering my anger around who had hurt me and looking at my shame and guilt around issues that didn't seem either safe or "correct" to talk about. I had decided to "play nice" and sweep my inner demons, of clinging to my ego, under the proverbial rug and it was clouding my spirit. Until I made the attempt to do that work, of naming it, talking about forgiveness and working on forgiveness became two different things.

But let me be honest, I didn't want to do the work of uncovering the layers of dirt that I used to bury all of my struggles. I have to admit all I wanted was a snappy finish to this journey so I could move on to the next great thing. I don't know about you, but in my life, I want a quick fix of anything I encounter, and that's just me being honest. Think of the products that we have created or the commercials that permeate our air waves.

- Dermablend Quick-Fix Concealer Natural
- Quick-Fix Vegetarian: Healthy Home Cooked Meals
- No Gray Quick Fix Instant Touch Up for Gray Roots
- Goldfaden MD Liquid Face Lift
- Quick Fix Urine (this one troubles me for some reason because I didn't even finish researching what that really means!)

But also, in our quick fix lives we have drive-thrus, pizza at our door in 30 minutes or less, the 15-minute oil change and even drive in church services, where you can sit in your car and they will put a speaker on your window!

These ideas around quick fixes have stopped us from doing the work. We have lost the traditional value of this basic principle, "nothing worth having comes easy." I don't think we recognize that there is a debate going on around ease or hard work. On top of that, I don't believe we acknowledge the power of the subliminal messages that are all around us.

The truth of the matter is, I could tell you clearly who hurt me, what day it was, the weather conditions and even what smells were in the air! I could recount it to anyone who would listen with great detail, as if it was a badge of honor to be displayed, not realizing it wasn't a badge at all but rather a noose. I wanted a quick fix to the forgiveness process. But there is no quick fix, there are moments when the universe whispers truths to us, that land in our bones, but there are no quick fixes.

In, *A Course in Miracles* or *ACIM*, it says, 'the holy instant is a miniature of eternity. It is a picture of timelessness, set in a frame of time[2].' It also says, 'In the holy instant nothing happens that has not always been. Only the veil that has been drawn across reality is lifted. Nothing has changed[3].' In an instant that is what happened to me. I knew that this holy instances happen was the universe whispering a truth, and it was then that I began to see people for who they truly are. It is when we see this world and all the illusions that have been concealing what has always been there, love and forgiveness or the Divine.

In 2012 I had gastric bypass surgery because I had skyrocketed to 283 pounds but prior to that I tried every quick fix weight loss program I could find. But nothing worked. My weight gain

---

[2] ACIM T-17.IV.11:4,5
[3] ACIM T-15.VI.6:1-3

tipped the scales, literally and figuratively, and things where so out of balance that my doctor said to me two things, "Imani, you have a 175% chance of dying at this rate (we all are at 100%) and quick fixes will never work." Then she said, "it took you years to put on the weight, why do you think you can just lop off 100 pounds in 3 months, it's not logical or safe."

How does this relate to the area of love, forgiveness and compassion? There are no quick fixes in this any of these areas, either. The fact of the matter is, that so often we just want to get high. We want a quick fix of heroin in our arms and that is not what the universe wants to do for us. What God wants, is to partner with us to change our hearts, renew our minds and open us to possibilities so that we can change, renew and open the world up to something beautiful.

However, there is an attitude adjustment that we need about many of these areas. Only then can our real selves be known. If we would stop and realize that we are safe with God and that our egos are in the midst of all of this telling us that we should or can fix things quickly, so to speak, we would realize it is just a waste of time.

HOW WE MET

I N NOVEMBER 2013 I HAD resigned myself to get back on Match. com, a dating website I had tried out in the past. I had been out on different dates in the months prior, but took myself off the site for a bit because, quite honestly, it was exhausting. Between the time it takes to correspond with people and the dates I did go on – let's just say, many times I had to challenge myself to even stay with the conversations or dates because these men had issues I normally would not have dealt with. For example there was one gentleman, and I use the term very loosely, we had decent enough conversations through the one on one communication online so I thought it would be a good time to give him my phone number and tell him about my profession as a pastor, that I found was a good barometer to who I was dealing with. Well, clearly the online communication was the just enough of a veil before he revealed his true colors. Within the first thirty minutes of the conversation on the phone I chose to tell him about my work, and the reason I typically hesitate is because I have such a public job and my hope is to weed out the crazies! I have since renamed him to "Coo-coo for Cocoa Puffs!"

The conversation went like this:

Me: So, I've been wanting to tell you about my work.

Coo-Coo: Yea, I'm really intrigued by you and what you do.

Me: Well, it's not that I was trying to be secretive but I just work in such a public forum I want to make sure you was cool.

Coo-Coo: I get it, theres a lot of nut jobs out there.

Me: Tell me about it! So… (he interrupts)

Coo-Coo: I bet you are like someone who works for the city, like in the mayors office or something.

Me: (I laugh) Not at all, I don't have the savvy for that kind of job. I actually am a pastor, the senior pastor of a church.

Coo-Coo: (pause)

Me: For some that's a deal breaker, I totally understand.

Coo-Coo: Not for me.

Me: Really? That's (he interrupts again)

Coo-Coo: Actually, it's always been a fantasy of mine.

Me: (in my head) What the fuck did he just say?

Coo-Coo: Yea, that's cool. I mean, would you ever have sex on the altar?

Me: I think this conversation is over. (CLICK)

So needless to say, my resignation is more than being picky. But I did meet some other gentleman that didn't live in crazy town. But unfortunately, out of the two guys I went out with several times, my mind or spirit was never challenged, and my prayer is that is not hurtful to anyone. However, I continued to give them a chance—until both of them at different times allowed me to exit gracefully.

The first gentleman thought I was really enamored with him and thought "I liked him too much" and the other gentleman said to me, "well, I would be attracted to you except you have that extra skin on your stomach." Well, let's just say both instances provided my out and I took it! Quickly!

You see, I have not been one that has connected easily with men. I've been in love or what I thought was love, once in my life and that was with my son's father, Paul, and after his murder—well, it just never clicked for me. In relationship to my daughter's father, I loved him to the best of my ability but the reality was I did not operate in a forgiven self so it was doomed from the beginning, not because of him but my own self. Did I experience love in some ways with others? Absolutely. It seems to be a part of my nature to be "loving" but it wasn't a love in the truest definition.

After Paul's death, there were a series of incidents in my life that moved me to be closed off in regards to relationships, unforgiving to both myself and others, creating this feeling of being hard of heart. With Paul's murder, grief manifested itself in me physically. The result was I gained an additional 160 pounds. I was trapped in this body and let it take over my very spirit. It was like I was stifled within this body and trying to slowly strangle myself. I didn't truly love others, or myself, I taught people about the importance of forgiveness but didn't truly understand or practice it within myself.

When Paul was murdered I struggled with guilt that was almost stifling. Paul and I had a relationship that was complicated at best. He and I loved each other, but he and I also knew how to fight like a Muhammad Ali and Joe Frazier match up.

Each fight was legendary.

From a quiet battle of words in the middle of a night club to the kicking in of my house door because he thought, I had someone in the house with me or whatever else he was thinking at the time. It was unhealthy to say the least. But I believe that Paul could confide in me like no one else. From his fears, indecencies, and inadequacies that seemed to plague his mind. But one thing was sure, he loved his son Hakeem and it began a turn in him. However that turn was too slow.

This was 1996 and the height of drugs, both being used and sold, seemed to hit a record high in Columbus Ohio. Paul and I had talked that Monday night about him coming to church with me the following week, and he asking if he could come over. I said, no. That is one "no" that seems to haunt me.

I could hear the desperation in his voice. He wanted to apologize for the huge blow up we had the week before and I wanted to let him in, again.

But, I couldn't.

I had to stop the cycle of abuse. So, I said, no. The early into the next morning, something didn't feel right, so I drove his hang out points. I discovered that Paul was found with stab wounds on Minnesota Ave, near the payphone he called me from.

From that point on, I found comfort in one place, food. Holding on to the guilt of "what if I said yes." What if I saw the true nature of Paul would he still be here for my son? So I ate… and ate. Abusing the body that was left behind. But within, I could hear a gentle calling beyond my ego to say, it's time to let it go. So after some time, I did.

In November 2013, as I said, I was back on Match.com and I remember seeing this profile of a man whose handle was, 'bbraski'. It intrigued me and even more so, his profile was full of nuggets that made me pause, because I knew he was intelligent and would challenge me in the most positive ways. In addition, he had a smile that lit my heart up.

Simultaneously, while I was corresponding with him online, I was taking yoga teacher training. During this, the owner Cyndi, of Breathe Yoga Studio, here in Rochester NY, took us through a practice that was geared towards forgiveness. In this 90 degree room, she asked each of us to make a list of who we needed to forgive. I remember my list: It just had one word: Myself.

I had no idea what that simple one word list would spark in me. Because as I moved through the asanas, which are yoga poses that the body forms, I started weeping and forgiveness flowed as I went through the following:

- I forgive myself for choosing sex without depth
- I forgive myself for choosing people I knew didn't have my best interest at heart and not caring enough for myself to choose otherwise
- I forgive myself for being in debt
- I forgive myself for not forgiving the man who murdered Paul

- I forgive myself for not always choosing forgiveness
- I forgive myself for how I have treated my body
- I forgive... I forgive....

And I swear something within me popped! It wasn't my hip, knee or back which usually happened during the poses in this then, 44 year old shell. Something opened up in me, and I began to see I was not this body, I was not my story, I was not my choices but rather I was a creature that was connected to the divine in more ways and I was not any more or any less than anyone else. My perspective changed in that moment.

Within the next week of "flirty" and "intellectually stimulating" banter with bbraski we met at a local bar. I remember not having any of the nervousness I had in the past, but rather an excitement to meet him. This excitement seemed to bubble up in me all that day. So that Tuesday, November 19th, I walked into the back door of the tavern, turned the corner and life as I knew it would never be the same.

THE CONVERSATION

AFTER WALKING INTO THE BACK door of the bar, I saw him. I mean, I saw bbraski, who I now know is Eric. I saw this man sitting very erect in his chair, and wearing a beautiful blue shirt that brought out his eyes. He smiled, and that same smile that lit me up within, just like it did when I saw his picture. His smile simply went through me, and I had to make a quick dash into the women's restroom before going over to the table. I gave him a motion of, 'one sec,' before going into the restroom and then did a little dorky dance behind closed doors.

Maybe I should explain that, it's that moment that you do your own version of a happy dance that you hope no one sees. Kinda like when, Chandler, on the show, "Friends," dances his little victory dance, not that Eric was something I "won" but just the goofiness of it all. It was really something, because while most of my friends would tell you that I'm not very girly, in that moment I became a schoolgirl grinning from ear to ear.

I pulled myself together walked out to the high table, and became very formal. I don't know why for certain, but it seemed to be what was called for in the moment. Maybe I was slightly afraid. It could have been my means of self-protection that I had chosen many times before, because of course there was the possibility that as soon as he saw me he would run for the door! But, we ordered beers and we went through the formalities. A giggle, a slight touch, and a compliment here and there. We talked about work, but not too much. He stayed sitting very upright and I tried to not let on that I was mush!

As we sat there talking, something in me truly saw him. I

19

don't know if you have ever had that feeling before. It may be another person that you are attracted to, a colleague, friend, someone in passing, but seeing someone and looking beyond the physical. It is a connection of the soul, and there is something that connects the two people, or the group of people, that is bigger than this earth plane. It was when I saw him, in that blue shirt, all kinds of bells seemed to go off in my head. Along with the bells were internal questions that seemed to become rapid fire:

- How do I know this man really?
- Have we met before?
- Is there truly something to soul mates?
- Did I tell him in another time and create what Dr. Weiss calls, "a soul plan" for him to wear that blue shirt because it is one of my favorite colors?

These questions swirled around in my head and I knew there was something more to this conversation. It was more than a flirt, a touch, and more than small talk. We truly took our time to get to know each other, and hear each other and our stories, while we sat at the high table.

A lesson that I've learned in my life is the, art of noticing, as well as the, art of seeing someone. This lesson is one I have carried with me even as I have conversations with others. I believe, in so many ways, we are connected to the next individual, and don't see it, or choose not to see it. For example, I was walking around yesterday in a local store and I watched people not make ANY eye contact with other people in the store, even the cashier. There was no sense that any other person was even there. People scrambled around to get their items, looked at the next thing, talked on their cell phones, and one by one, no one saw the other. Most didn't even notice what was happening around them.

One of the beauties of yoga is it teaches you how to be present in whatever moment you are in. Yoga calls you to feel what is going on with you in your body, and bring your focus to whatever is going on in your heart. Yoga calls you to notice. It is more than feeling the body from the standpoint of nailing the poses, it's more about how can you take what you learn on your mat, off your mat.

This reminds me of another moment while I was in yoga teacher training, Carly, one of the trainers, led us through an exercise that was very powerful and reminded me of my time with Eric, and how I, now, try to see others. What we did, all 42 of us in teacher training, was walk around the room in a serpentine fashion, without talking, and then when we heard the words, we stopped and would face the person that was in front of us and just stare at them. No laughter, no words, just look at them. The first time we moved through the room and we stopped before the other person, I was paired with a gentleman in the class. We stared into each others eyes, and I noticed him to begin to cry. When asked what it was he felt, he wondered about all those things that may have broken my fragile heart. The second time through the exercise I was paired with a young woman who was typically, very bubbly, and I wondered about her true story and if she saw that she was more than what society kept telling her she was or wasn't. Both incidents were incredibly powerful. You begin to see the creases in a person's face, you begin to wonder why those creases are in their face, you begin to wonder about this person's journey and you look deep into their eyes and attempt to touch their souls. For some, it made them tear up, others it made them full of joy. People truly saw each other for the first time.

The lesson that I take from my conversation with Eric is how I need to do that with everyone I meet. Not just someone that I see as beautiful with eyes that make you melt, but see every person as another soul.

Dave Chappelle has a bit in his comedy special that I especially love. I am not going to get the joke exactly right but I think you will get my point. He says,

"Sesame Street has fucked up our children! That's right I said it. Take Oscar the Grouch for example. The kids see Oscar and they say, 'Oscar you're a grouch!' Of course he is, he's the poorest motherfucker on Sesame Street! He lives in a garbage can! And we wonder why our kids grow up and step over homeless people and say, 'get a job, grouch!"

The point behind that, is that many times people no longer see people. They no longer take time to connect, even for a moment, unless it has something for them in it.

How can we take the lesson of who we love, our family, spouse, whoever, and translate it into how we begin to see each other. The conversation with Eric was life changing. It can be the same for all of us if we take the time to let it. In the midst of this talk I knew it was going to be something that would change my life, and—for all intent and purposes—it did.

ONE SHOT KILL

E RIC HAS SPENT THE LAST 26 years in the army reserves. Our first conversation hinted towards what he does in the military, but he made sure he didn't give me too much information. He did however, tell me that there was no chance that he would be going off to war. Needless to say, that was a relief. I couldn't imagine in that moment him being away from me. Maybe he saw it on my face, a small concern of sorts, even though we just met. Those hints of what he did in the military were not filled with a lot of details. Which was ok, because as far as he knew, I could have been some crazy stalker girl! But, he was open to the possibility that I was not.

The other thing he spent a considerable amount of years doing is teaching elementary age kids. That gave me pause, and it showed, even though he wasn't trying to show this to me a softness in him. He had a look of seriousness behind his eyes, or maybe it was a searching. It was like he didn't want to give me too much information, and maybe it wasn't some fear that I was the crazy stalker girl, but more of quieting his own ego and allowing whoever he was sitting across from to see him as the soul, who is just on this journey like the rest of us.

He was beautiful to watch and I don't mean that purely from a physical perspective. He was clear and concise with his words, you could tell he liked the nuances of a good tete-a-tete! Along with that, he spoke and moved with intentionality. He was well read and non judgmental. He had a gentle yet strong presence. It was truly majestic, and beautiful, and I don't mean that in hindsight. I remember thinking it while we talked. I didn't want the date to end, and I don't think he did either. But I think we purposely made this date on a weekday to kind of cover ourselves for a possible escape. So as we parted ways, I felt an overwhelming feelings of excitement, surprise, happiness, and even love begin to take over me. I shook it off, so I thought.

Now, as I said, we met on Match.com and so of course there were different people we both were talking to. I had a couple of dates lined up with people that were pretty surface and easy to read. One was a bar owner in the area and I agreed to go watch a game at his establishment. He was nice enough, but there were no "take my breath away" moments, and he was a young soul, you could tell by his conversation and his very carnal way of looking at things. I was kind and charming but my mind drifted the entire time.

Then there was another date. We met at a coffee house. He worked security for a hospital and was very nice kind, gentle, church going, he loved his family, but something happened not even half way through this date, I drifted so far away that I couldn't help but say to him, "I'm sorry, I can't do this." He looked confused and so I followed it up with, "I met someone the other night and I just have to…" He gave a gentle smile, we hugged and I immediately went out to the car, called Eric and asked if he would like to meet for a bite and a drink. And even though it was 8:00 on a school night, he said "yes!"

When we arrived at the restaurant, I was bubbling with excitement and that feeling that was overwhelming me on our first date was there warming me and flooding my senses. Seeing his smile, to this day, takes me back to that moment. We ate, and talked, and I told him how grateful I was for him coming out to see me. He told me how he thought of me, and I did the same.

It was then I learned the phrase, "one shot kill," from the military. That's what had happened. We both had been shot by the universe at this moment in time. To learn a lesson, or many lessons, but one of love for sure. A love for not only each other but love that is to be demonstrated for others to see and practice. A love that has a certain type of order.

As we finally decided to part ways for the night, we stood in the street face to face and when he placed his arms around me and I looked up into his eyes, those feelings of gratitude, happiness, excitement, and love again ran over me like a dam bursting. He kissed me and I swear the entire world was drowned in that feeling and we left this place called earth.

One shot kill is right!

In that moment some things began to die. I stood upright and was strong in my footing, and so was he. But what ended up laying on the ground after that shot was how we would see the world. Because the chalk line was forming and laying inside of it was judgment, hatred, fear and ego. And we would never be the same.

THE KISS

A FTER SEVERAL MOMENTS OF WANTING to kiss him, from the first time I saw him, we did. I guess this portion of the book is more like a, Quentin Torentino, movie because I'm telling you about the kiss first and then going backwards. As we stood out in the street beside the restaurant, without any concern for anyone else in the world, we kissed. I remember it was like breathing for the first time, and I remembered nothing, and everything all at once. If rainbows and unicorns could have shot out from certain orifices of our bodies – I'm sure that would have happened as well, because it was more than a kiss. It was like I was home for a moment, unlike any home I remember in this lifetime. But a home I knew I belonged to.

It felt like it was a moment that the whole world stood went in slow motion and I noticed the breath moving through my nostrils and the sound of my heart beating smoothly. It was a moment that I felt the holy show up. My guarded persona didn't show up, and it was like I walked into the door of a place I ran away from, and I was the prodigal daughter being welcomed back. This home was one that I knew, in that moment, if only for a moment, and it was a place where I was whole, healed, and basking in the glow of the love of God. Now that's a kiss.

My ego shut off, and stopped screaming words at me of what I was supposed to be or who I was not. It was as if there was no time at all, and within that moment, I experienced joy. A joy that was unspeakable. There is no better way to say it, time stood still, is the best way to describe this sacred moment between the two of us. I felt it truly in every part of my body, and it wasn't sexual, or even lust-filled. It was home.

So often we refer to our bodies and how our bodies feel in any given moment. Usually how we feel in our body determines how we will respond to a situation or a person. From, she turns me on, or he makes me feel like a "natural woman!" Or the opposite, he makes me sick, or she gives me the creeps. All determine our actions and our responses to the person, but what about how we respond to ourselves? What tapes does it replay in our mind about who we are? We tend to allow people to determine what we see in ourselves versus the truth of our essence.

One my my mantras in meditation is three simple words. I. Am. Love. For me that reinforces the truth that I am healed. I am whole. That I am shining God's love in the world. That I am fearless. That I am joy.

You see, in this kiss, I started to get a glimpse of what my true identity is by realizing what it was not. It was not:

- Someone who had to have a companion
- Someone who was a single mother
- Someone who was victimized
- Someone who was a pastor
- Someone who was a woman
- Someone who used to be extremely overweight
- Someone who is not overweight
- Someone who is a yogi
- Someone who...

None of those descriptors that used to give me title or that had been identifiers were true in that moment. Every illusion that I lived in and had let guide me was totally obliterated and I watched the things that I lived in as "what I am" shatter.

And it was beautiful.

In that moment I realized I was what the scriptures state, ' just as he chose us in Christ before the foundation of the world to be holy and blameless before him in love.[4]' Or as it says in the Yoga Sutras, "Then the seer becomes established in its true nature[5]." This assurance that I am love, is not an ego thing because the ego would love for me to live just in what I have designated as MY story of identifiers that are just labels that we have created. Our ego and the images that we project on ourselves and each other would rather we forget these ancient truths of being chosen, safe with God, true nature and that we are messengers. No, the truth is, the universe, and the Divine is always trying to point us to the truth of who we all really are. We are spirits or souls that are home, safe with God.

[4] Ephesians 1:4
[5] Yoga Sutra 1.3

A Time for Meditation:

So often, we loose ourselves in others. It starts off innocently enough, doing activities that the person likes or eating food that otherwise you know you don't enjoy. That very clear decision to not be authentically ourselves, although pure in intention, is like a gateway drug to loosing our voice and in essence our very selves. Changing to fit in never truly fits. You are created the way you are for a reason.

In your meditation time today, allow the memory of your greatest happiness, that originates within you stir up excitement and love so that it can be like a dam bursting forth within, as you recite the lovingkindness meditation.

May I be happy
May I be well
May I be safe
May I be peaceful

Part 2

A TINY MAD IDEA OR TMI

I N THE MIDST OF TALKING to my children about different issues as they grew up, sometimes I would use real experiences of my life to give them an example of how to move through their situation. Inevitably, I would talk to my son about, "what a girl likes," or to my daughter about, "what a boy likes," and they would shout out with fingers in their ears, "TMI mom!" This "too much information" that they hated to hear from me, at times was intentional, just to mess with my children and be a little tortuous. I had to get some kicks somewhere with them. But many times it was to provide them with a safe place where they could tell me anything, and I wanted to be an example of that.

I've recently heard about another TMI but it stands for the Tiny Mad Idea that essentially is that we believe, as beings here in this time and place are separated from each other and from a power greater than ourselves, as well as, ourselves. While, choosing this thought results in what we are experiencing as our lives as bodies in the physical universe and everything just fells like an illusion and out of sorts. But the truth of the matter is, each of us, are safe and truly home with God. In that way, maybe *Too Much Information* and *Tiny Mad Idea* could be synonymous with each other.

The interconnectedness of all of humanity, the earth, the world and with the divine seems to be lost on us. We are so committed to the illusion that we are separate from each other and that our actions or lack of actions means anything to the next person or this world. We are not separate form God. None of us are more special than another. We each have purpose.

For far to long, what I have begun to realize is that I have been sold a bill of goods. Whether it is ideas about ourselves, another person or the world. We believe we are separated from God and we are living out a separate reality from God. That is the tiny, mad idea.

All the things that we think are important or, "real," is so far from true, yet it is what we end up believing. That's why we obsess over issues that have no life giving properties. For example, we believe that we are separated from God. But nothing separates us from God. Not even our own nonsense. The truth of the matter is, we are all home safe with God.

Think of it from this angle, in two different places, (and there are others but I would just like to focus on these two) we read scripture and say the following:

"And I give unto them eternal life; and they shall never perish, neither shall any man pluck them out of my hand. My Father, which gave them me, is greater than all; and no man is able to pluck them out of my Father's hand."[6] and "For I am convinced, that neither death, nor life, nor angels, nor principalities, nor powers, nor things present, nor things to come, Nor height, nor depth, nor any other creature, shall be able to separate us from the love of God, which is in Christ Jesus our Lord.[7]"

Both of these scriptures have been a source of comfort for people over the centuries. Why is it that, we can hold fast to this truth and not believe we are safe in God's hands, but rather that we are just working through our stuff, free will, or maybe salvation? Why would a loving God allow us to be truly in harms way? This dream, of sorts, we have created is that we are out of God's hand, but we are not. And because of that we are fearful, angry, full of doubt, hesitancy and regret while we hold on to the things that we believe we should have aversion to. What I have

---

[6] John 10:28-29
[7] Romans 8:38-39

realized is that it is time to let that go. To welcome my true self and the true selves of others and not to fear. It's like a voice that calls, not only me, but all of us to waken to love without fear.

I am sick and tired of what the church overall has told us about who God is. The church has become an outer monologue of our ego tells us that if we go back to God, He will destroy us. It is this fear of God's wrath that continually impels us to maintain a perpetual state of not being mindful of how we live our lives. It's like the muscle memory within our brain is dormant and we have forgotten true deep truths about ourselves. That is the egos defense mechanism so that we can stay waddled up in our shit.

I think this is a very limited view of how Christians see God. That we would be destroyed by God is contrary to who God is. This isn't mine or Lutheran, that God will destroy me or anyone for that matter. I believe firmly that God is loving of everyone, no matter what. And as scripture says in Romans 8, "nothing can separate us from the love of God."

- Do I think we all have some primordial fear that we will be judged, so we try to hide ourselves from God? Yes.
- Do I believe that our egos are screaming in our heads that we could never be loved fully and accepted by God? Yes.
- Do I believe that we perpetuate the tiny mad idea, that we are not safe in God's hand? Yes.
- Do I think that God allows us to have free will to do this? Yes.

So is this all a dream? Yes, but not from the perspective of Bobby Ewing waking up in the shower, and all the twists and turns of the previous season of Dallas being just his imaginings. (By the way, that had to be a long shower!) But from the perspective that the dream is that God would allow any harm to truly come to us. Harm that would keep us from God. Forever. The dream and, tiny mad idea, is God does not love us. You see, there is another story that is full of so much loving kindness, and that is, the universe, that God, that your higher self wants you to be happy, peaceful, healthy and kind. God doesn't want anyone to be alone and He wants us back home.

However we can't get there until we practice forgiveness of ourselves and others. But that can only happen once we begin to truly understand our true identity and recognize the harm that we do constantly do our selves.

BREWERIES, BOOKS AND BABBLINGS

A S I GOT TO KNOW Eric, our conversations together were the combination of not so random thoughts about beer, books, travel, work, and even the craziness we had seen in ourselves, our family, and all around us. It truly was many days of babbling about different topics that didn't seem to stop, even when it was 4 a.m. I thought for sure we would eventually run out of things to talk about, or some uneasiness would happen, especially on our first mini road trip. So what did I do, I made a playlist to fill the empty space, to fill the silence. I didn't want those uncomfortable silences to stop these wonderful moments. I was discovering with this kind soul, that I felt I'd known for so much longer than I did.

My playlist included the following songs that would hopefully stimulate how much he adored me even before he knew it! (Don't act like you have never done that when you were sitting in the car with someone and you put on that perfect song that helps awaken a moment!) The playlist was appropriately entitled, "The Drive," and periodically I listen to it because it almost feels prophetic. The songs included:

- I Try - Ben Taylor
- It's A Man's, Man's World - James Brown
- I Won't Give Up & You Fckn Did It - Jason Mraz
- Just My Imagination - The Temptations
- Let's Get It On - Marvin Gaye
- Pour Some Sugar On Me - Def Leppard

Ok, you get it… maybe I should have left off songs like, "Let's Get It On and Pour Some Sugar On Me," now that I think about it, but hey, the list was made nonetheless.

Well, I got into the car to head out to, Abandon Brewery, with Eric. I was greeted with a gentle kiss that made me smile as big as a Cheshire Cat. As I sat down, the discussions we had over the phone and via email seemed to just pick up. There was not any of the awkwardness I had anticipated. I was comfortable in my skin, and he was in his. There was no fear in our interactions from the very beginning. However my mind, my silly little ego, tried to get me to move into that modality I was slowly leaving behind. It was like, the ego, was playing the movie, *"The Godfather,"* in my mind, and it left a horse head in my bed to terrify me.

However, instead of moving into the fear, I chose to do something different. I chose to listen to a very small voice deep inside of me, rather than the, loud banging pans like a toddler, ego that typically made me run in fear. I chose to see both of us as old friends, or maybe even deeper as old souls, and see both of us in that moment as we drove to met two of his friends.

We met up at the brewery for the first time, with friends of his, Mike and Mykel, who are husband and wife. I had a moment of, "oh holy cow what if they don't like me," but again that was a tape trying to move me from the truth of myself. Without giving into those thoughts, I wanted to be the same person I had been with him, with the two of them. So I was. From gentle touches to Eric's back, laughing goofily, talking about matters of faith, work, and whatever came to mind. In those moments, I saw them not as strangers I just met, but as beautiful souls.

One of my favorite quotes from ACIM is 'Fear is a stranger to the ways of love. Identify with fear, and you will be a stranger to yourself.[8]' I think the reason I have been drawn to this quote is because of my Aunt Jwahir and Aunt Azuka, the twins of

---

[8] ACIM - W-PI.160.1.1–2

the family, always referred to this indirectly by an acronym they taught me when I was younger. F.E.A.R. - False Evidence Appearing Real. They would spout it off before I took a test, went to a new school, tried a new food, or met new people. There where a number of times they threw that acronym around to help me move past my inner battle of fear.

You see, if I would have stayed in my fear, which is the acronym - false evidence appearing real, then I would have let my inner dialogue move me instead of trying to walk in the true self that is at home with God. The other part was, seeing them as I saw myself, as innocent and full of love no matter what I knew about them. We fell into a rhythm that seemed natural. Not one of us was trying to impress the other, or judge with the eyes but instead we wanted goodness, peace, and a great beer!

Fear is a mad dog at times, it will come up and bite you like the dog it is, without any regret. Actually it may be even worse. It is a life truck that slams you in the intersection without warning. My hope is to strip away all aspects of fear in my life. To move as if it's nonexistent. I wonder what life would be like if we all did that? I wonder if we can begin to strip away the fear? What ever it is for us, that creates the FALSE EVIDENCE (that) APPEARS REAL.

For me, on that day, it was feelings of inadequacies that I have stored away from the days of my childhood, that tried to nag me into old tapes. Whether it was because of the childhood banter of "light, bright, and damn near white" that made me feel unaccepted by those that were black or the harsh words of my high school boyfriend's father that said, "how can you kiss those coon lips," there were moments that tried to keep me from the true identity and the joy that I had come to know about myself and this life and not what others have tried to imply.

Do you remember cassette tapes? I do. I remember getting mix tapes of music from boyfriends they made for me. A mash-up of their feelings. One even gave me a break-up mix tape and for years I couldn't listen to the song, *"Owner of a Lonely Heart,"* without recalling how much of a jerk move it was! But this is how cassette tapes work, "the tape (in the cassette) moves against the head (of the tape recorder) and either records or plays sounds due to the electromagnet rearranging of the particles or disorienting the particles in the case of the recording."[9] But what I think is important to note is the similarity of what cassette tapes do and what the tapes in our minds do - *they disorient.* Messages that we play in our head over and over again are disoriented realities. For example, if you play back a cassette tape you usually sound a little warped or you hear little fuzzy sounds in the recording. But the reality is your voice that is on the tape usually isn't as bad as we think we sound, or something we think we hear is non-existent. Also, the quality of what we hear is usually poor. But the other thing about cassette tapes that I find similar to our playing of the tapes in our mind is when we play a cassette tape too often, it usually unwinds to a mess, leaving us with the job of having to try to re-wind the tape into the case so we can play it over and over again. I think it's time to throw out those cassettes. They never worked well in the first place. And neither does the tape in our minds.

---

[9] www.web.bryant.edu

ANOTHER LIFE

B EYONCE HAS A SONG CALLED, "Ego," it discusses the concept within our society about how a man has often thought his identity was wrapped in what his, "package," can do. That's why we have the grabbing of crotches while making the rude gestures that follow. Now, before I get accused of bashing men, because that is not what this is, we as women do the same thing. We have also defined ourselves with the power of what is between our legs. Like the Summers Eve commercial that proclaims, "power to the V," and it shows men kneeling everywhere. It all points to our ego, this identity of what we believe defines us.

There are a few things that the ego would have us believe:

1. That we define ourselves and we are better than another.
2. That we are not safe in the hand of God.
3. That we are unforgivable and we have believed we are something we are not.

We, as a people, have grasped ahold of being a victim, unforgiving, hate-filled, and vengeful instead of walking in the image of the love that we are created in.

Originally I was going to call this book, "Waking Sleeping Beauty." The premise was initially going to be how the "ego" puts the Christ in us to sleep and the Holy Spirit leads the Prince of Forgiveness to place a holy kiss to wake us up. Then I thought, that is a pretty arrogant title, and kind of dorky, sprinkled with cheesiness. Arrogant to the point of getting wrapped into the physicality of the self, and dorky because it points to my weird love of some Disney shows. But the truth of the matter is, I have realized that we are so caught up in the physicality of it all. When the reality is that this body's job is to help us experience the truth of who we are called to be.

I know the thought of past lives can get a little crazy in our minds and many theologies renounce the idea as blasphemy. I also want to clarify that I am by no means and expert on the topic. But this is what I am beginning to believe…that we all come back, over and over again, trying to get it right. Not trying to find that perfect soul mate but rather soul mates that are a part of the plan to heal the ego and misalignment that we have created in this world. The, "bill of goods," that we have sold ourselves is the idea that the prince will come, and we will magically get a kiss and live happily ever after, but that is very one sided and self serving. That type of soul mate is not helping anyone but our own individual need to feel special. But rather, what if soul mates (yes plural) was the real idea that leads us to our true identity.

Soul mates are the people you naturally gravitate to. Those who just push your buttons to go a little further and a little deeper. What if those people have been with you for decades, trying to get you to live out your soul plan of bringing light and love into this world? What if these soul mates show up as your teacher, mailman, next door neighbor, best friend, spouse, or even nemesis. They are there, not to let you just have it easy and comfortable, but rather to push you towards your higher self. That's why love isn't "special" it just is.

Eric and I did a past life regression and this is what I've discovered. I've come back and will come back again, and again, to try and convince the world to be more compassionate, loving, and practice forgiveness. You will do the same, some way or another with that same purpose in mind. Because that's really what all of life is really about. To be more compassionate, loving and forgiving. Look at the lives that have had a profound change on the world that invites us to do something different that frees us from our egos. Great sages like, Buddha, Mother Theresa, Dr. Martin Luther King, Gandhi, or Jesus.

MY AUNTS BOOK SHELF

GROWING UP I REMEMBER THIS blue book on the shelf of my, Aunt Azuka's, house. It was titled, *A Course in Miracles*. Jump to me as an adult, I remember someone gave me a copy of the book and I kept it on my shelf, looking at periodically but not really studying the book, or reading it for extended periods of time. About three years ago I picked it up again and started reading sections. Not that I studied it by any means, but my interest was peaked, especially recalling that I had seen this book most of my life growing up. It had survived time.

You can imagine my surprise when Eric brought up the book during one of our dates. He was cooking dinner for us and as I stood across the island in his kitchen, he asked me if I had ever heard of *that same book*. I smiled, and said yes. He was surprised because it was something he had only recently come across. I told him, it was something that was always around growing up. Within a few days, we started reading it individually at our own pace, and he would tease me about eventually becoming a course teacher within my role as a pastor. I was just happy to find a safe place to discuss this book and still am.

Now let me be clear, I'm not by any means an expert on the religious texts, but I have found profound truths to bring into my life, along with scriptures, and even my yoga practice. Truth is truth. I especially love, and have highlighted and gone back to this quote, 'Miracles reawaken the awareness that the spirit, not the body, is the altar of truth. This is the recognition that leads to the healing power of the miracle.[10]

What is the miracle? It's not some magic trick and it's not simply about healing—like being able to hear, walk, or no longer have cancer. The true meaning of a miracle is moving away from the fear our mind would like us to hold on to. The miracle is removing that fear so we are no longer strangers to ourselves, and instead undo what the fear has limited us to, and from. When we begin to recognize who we truly are, that we are spiritual beings and that we are all connected to God, that's when the miracles occur. That means, we will then learn how to be love, give love, and express that love though forgiveness, not only to others, but even to ourselves for believing something we are not. You see, the miracle is practicing love and forgiveness.

If we could do that, that would be a miracle. It would free us from fear and truly undo all the nonsense that we have created within this world. To some extent I understand why I couldn't read *ACIM* when I was 17, 21, 26, or even in my 30's. It's because I was too busy trying to acquire more, take advantage of situations, life, or even the wish to hold onto grudges. Because as I discussed earlier about the ego, I believed I was the captain of my own ship, but the reality was, I was the captain of my own shit! Now I see all of those moments in my life as things that have influenced and guided me, to see that the gathering of more stuff, or the holding onto my stuff is not necessary. To live a life of love and forgiveness is all this life should be about.

---

[10] ACIM - T-1.I15.1-2

45

A Time to Meditate:

On the back of a comic book growing up was an advertisement for sea monkeys. These creatures lived under the water and was having a grand time. They built cities, enjoyed a little underwater drink and laughed all day long. I wanted these sea monkeys. For $1.25 I could train a family of sea monkeys and the cartoon image of the family looking on at the aquirium gave me hope that would be my family of monkeys. So, when the package came and I dumped the dried bits of brine shrimp into the water and waited, and waited and waited some more, I realized that I had been duped. No sea monkeys ever grew and I was out of my allowance.

I could have let that bad experience with one company stop me from ever purchasing another item. That would have been a said state of events. It would have been limiting in my life. Then why do we let any bad event stop us from loving and believing, as well as, forgiving and offering grace. It's time to heal the rift and lie that we have perpetuated. It's time to realize, life happens and we will experience sorrow. But we can not stop living the life we are called to.

In your meditation time today, look for ways you can find your happy, as you recite the lovingkindness meditation.

May I be happy
May I be well
May I be safe
May I be peaceful

Part 3

CHRISTMAS MIRACLES

E RIC AND I, AS A couple, bought our first Christmas tree this year. Well, I bought our first Christmas tree. It was a small tabletop tree that smelled of fresh fir and it was just enough. Now, for me I have a history of doing Christmas up big! I buy a big tree, put up Christmas decorations from my kids past, and new ones for the year, add lights and more lights everywhere. I also have a thing for snowmen and have a collection of animated snowmen at my house. So to get a small tabletop tree with a man who had not one decoration in his house, was a bit of a challenge initially. But once I bought this tree, and brought it to his house, it fit. More than fitting the house, as most would think we needed a bigger tree based on the size of the room, no, it fit us.

While I was out, I picked up a ceramic pot, a table dressing, mini lights, and Eric's first Christmas decoration from me, a melted snowman! It seemed perfect because we both have these horrendous childhood memories of melted or decapitated snowmen that today make us laugh. So as the tree is being set up, Eric looks at it and says, "is that tree crooked?" And sure enough it was a crooked little tree that was almost as pathetic as Charlie Brown's Christmas tree and all we needed was a red bulb to have it lean over even more! So there we stood on this cold Christmas night, with the fire burning, taking in the imperfections of this tree.

In yoga you will hear all kinds of talk about how to make the pose perfect, and for some instructors that means making the pose look like a yoga magazine. But that's kind of ludicrous if you think about it. I am not the same height, body type, and I

49

don't have the same life experiences lived out in this body, as the person creating the shape of any particular pose they seem to nail in whatever magazine you happen to be reading. Besides, who knows how many times they had to shoot that person to get it "perfect." However, I love when an instructor will say that the pose is, "perfect," in your body however it looks. Yes, there are alignment cues, and things that you do to protect your body from injury, but it does land how it should for you differently each day.

ACIM lesson 67 starts off with the heading, "Love Created Me Like Itself." Doesn't that one statement just land in your body, mind and spirit in a powerful way? It does for me. *Love created me like itself.* Which leads to a natural deduction - if God is love then I am created like God, and if I am created like God then I am love, and if I am love then I can't be intolerant or hate. That is a pretty perfect revelation of identity. No matter who it is or what they look like, what their experiences are or what they will experience. They may be a crooked little tree but even that crooked little tree is made in the image of the Divine's love.

When our friends Mike and Mykel came over to enjoy the hot tub, drink a bottle of wine, or a beer or two, laugh and have a good time, Mykel walked over to our tree and said, "look at this beautiful little love tree." This crooked tree, with one string of lights, and one ornament, radiated love and the love that filled this house and even more so, each of us and the love we wanted to share with others.

Lesson 67 in *ACIM* says, 'Holiness created me holy. Kindness created me kind. Helpfulness created me helpful. Perfection created me perfect.[11]' We are made in that image. To be holy, kind, helpful, and perfect. Anything outside of that is not in the image of the One that we are called to reflect. That is unchangeable as *ACIM* talks about in various chapters. That's the reality that we need to remind ourselves.

---

[11] ACIM - W-PI.67.2-6

50

So the miracle of Christmas was that realization that we are all holy, kind, helpful, and perfect. It's like the book, *The Help* where, Abilene, the maid of a family was trying to teach the little girl Mobley, who she was helping to raise. Whenever Mobley felt insecure or was crying, Abiline would say that she was kind, special, and important. Maybe our mantra should be similar, "I am holy, I am kind, I am helpful, and I am perfect" so that we can move from our insecurities and see who we truly are.

Love.

NEW YEAR

I HAVE BEEN GOING THROUGH THE text messages that Eric and I have exchanged with each other since we first met. One of the series of text conversations that we were having was around me being ill from all the food I consumed in a short period of time. Here is the conversation:

Eric: Good morning beautiful :)

Me: What a way to bring a smile to my face. Good morning to you.

Me: Confession: I ate like shit yesterday because I was bummed - I have a food hangover!

Eric: What did u have?

Me: I ate a peanut butter and jelly sandwich big mistake; because that set off a sugar rush in me or something - then I had cheese and crackers probably 3-5 of them; then I had an apple with 2 tablespoons of caramel sauce; 1/2 curried chicken spring roll and of course 1 tablespoon of cookie butter. My body hates me right now I don't eat that much in a week. LOL

Eric: Wow... that is a lot 4 u. R U doing Ok with things today?

Things where not ok. A little background regarding my food limitations. Because of my gastric bypass I can't consume that much food, let alone sugar, because it creates a "dumping" syndrome that is painful, it makes me feel terrible, and I am not myself. I took out my anger, grief, frustration, pain, and a plethora of other negative feelings that I was struggling with, out on myself. I paid the piper within my body, because subconsciously I wanted to punish myself for experiencing joy.

ACIM says, 'The body represents the gap between the little bit of mind you call your own and all the rest of what is really yours...Sickness is anger taken out upon the body, so that it will suffer pain.'[12] I have been struggling within myself, for years perpetuating this idea and at some point and time, we all must get tired of it.

Whether it is *ACIM*, the *Bible*, or the *Sutras* there is language about our interconnectedness with each other, and with God. However, we continually separate ourselves from each other by creating labels of division, whether it's who is better, worse, black or white, rich or poor, or whatever the distinction. These separations reflect some vow that we all subconsciously have taken, which spurs wars, and rumors of wars, internally and around us. It creates special love relationships and historical hatreds. All ways in which we oppose who God has created us to be.

When I look back on what I did to my body, the first part of the New Year, it was wrapped up in insanity. My ego was telling me all kinds of things during that time period which point to Eric's question, "are you ok?" My ego was telling me I was not "ok" by saying things like:

- "So you're in love? You know he secretly hates your body."
- "So you're going to be in a magazine? You're a fraud."
- "So you are becoming a yoga teacher... um you do know that you have the worst hips ever and to top it off all those young girls are much better at it than you."
- "So you wrote a grant and of course you didn't get it!"

All things to separate me from love. Love from myself, love of another and love to be given out to the world. It was a ridiculous tape that was running in my head during that time period, and

---

[12] ACIM - T-28.VI.4:1

I thought I had to punish myself through food! So I broke my promise never to do that to myself. Yet again.

Ephesians 4:4 says, 'There is one body and one Spirit...' and yet we think that we can be separate from each other and from God. *The Course* compliments that text by saying 'let this be your agreement with each one; that you be one with him and not apart. And he will keep the promise that you make him, because it is the one that he has made to God, as God has made to him. God keeps His promises; His Son keeps his.[13]'

You see, the way I create sickness in my body, as if it is separate from me, is the same way I perpetuate sickness with others. It is the way we agree to attack and be attacked. It is the reoccurring theme of our lives that prohibits us from experiencing the joy we all have access too. This idea that, what we want is to suffer a little bit, because we have created some kind of secret vow as a way to punish ourselves, again and again. However, our true identity is not that we are in opposition to God and we are not in opposition of others. Rather, that we are in line with God and each other. We have just forgotten.

---

[13] ACIM - T-28.VI.6:1

RECOVERING BODY

I AM REALLY GOOD AT PLAYING the victim role. I can replay past hurts, and sit comfortably in it, and use it to manipulate details to fit what I want. It has the potential to show up as emotional blackmail, and I can hold people up for ransom, and hijack their life, and in turn my own life.

I mentioned this earlier, in the midst of the past four years I have lost a considerable amount of weight. 187 pounds to be exact! Between having gastric bypass surgery, lots of yoga, and some more yoga, I am grateful for this new body, so that I can journey here a little longer. However, I tend to get stuck when I feel judged. Let me be clear that I know it is based on the stuff that they are dealing with but it gets me stuck at times nonetheless. In the midst of losing weight, as you can imagine, I had some extra skin laying around different parts of my body. However I was proud of the weight that I had lost, what this body could do now, and really didn't pay the stomach skin too much mind.

Until, some time ago I went out with a guy that had a lot to say about my stomach skin. He said, "can you do something about that?" As I looked down to the belly he was pointing at, I paused and said, "well, after losing over 100 pounds that happens." He then said, "but that turns me off." My response in that moment was, "well your words just did the same thing to me, you can leave my porch now."

He was shocked.

I didn't care.

He left.

However, something clicked inside of me. The over

obsessing about this skin, and my ego went into overdrive about what was, "wrong with me." I worked out like a bandit and cut back even more on my eating. I even tried this, "saran wrap," and natural gel stuff to try to get rid of the excess skin, that felt like it was forever talking back to me, mocking me and yes, judging.

Until one day I felt pain in my side that just wouldn't go away. After a trip to the doctor, I discovered I had cysts that needed to be removed. Nothing life threatening but it truly put things in perspective. As soon as I began to forgive this voice in my head, or my belly, and that guy, opportunities presented themselves for me to heal. After minor surgery, and some major surgery that included a tummy tuck I still heard the ridicule within. It was slight but there and I had to practice quieting that voice, again and again. And now, I have buried that voice. Not because of the surgery, but because I started to realize what I wanted, and it wasn't a flat stomach. It was forgiveness. Forgiveness, first with myself, for the abuse I put my body through, or even the abuse I put myself mentally through. Because of forgiveness a realizing happened that I was projecting all types of negative feelings around me. From that point I read these words pretty much everyday:

Forgiveness offers everything I want.
Today I have accepted this as true.
Today I have received the gifts of God.

The problem is not your body, it wasn't my problem. The problem is not something or someone outside of you. The problem is not the political system. The problem is not your job. The problem is not your neighbor. The problem, if that is the word we choose, is what we have not forgiven in ourselves and how we are projecting it onto all of the scenarios that are bringing us angst. Dr. Luskin's last step is something we all have to remember, 'Amend your grievance story to remind you of the heroic choice to forgive.' And it's something that we may have to do every day. Just so our body, our mind, our ego and our projections can recover.

ADORE AND LOVE

E RIC SAID HE ADORED ME before he said anything about love. That confused me at first. No one had ever told me that they adored me, but I found it beautiful because of the implications of the word. This simple word adore was another step to me healing and experiencing the miracle of forgiveness.

The word adore has implications around honoring or to regard with the utmost respect and admiration. To adore is the opposite of abhorring. When we begin to look at something, or someone, with adoration we truly begin to look at them and take them in just as they are. Something about that began to release me from the guilt I had carried for years, around ways I had not always adored myself because of the choices I made within the illusion of thinking I was less. Because I made certain choices, whether it was promiscuity, lying about insignificant things, or even my spending habits to cover insecurities, I created within myself this idea that I wasn't *adorable*.

In this society we equate, adorable, to cute little dolls, pageant girls, or a little boys in tuxedos. But if we look at the origin of the word we can begin to be free from the judgement we place upon ourselves. Eric's adoring, helped me begin to see myself as more than the story I created.

Truth moment: I struggle with money, from saving it to spending it. I constantly sabotage myself to not have enough. I am always lacking in that department. From giving it all away, purchasing something for someone else or even something for myself, to give the illusion that I am *more* in their eyes. Instead of seeing that I don't have to do any of that, it has become apart of my story that keeps me in the unhealthy cycle of debt and scrambling. If I am honest, it is the thought that I am not enough, and not worthy of being looked at with respect and admiration. Why is that so important, respect and admiration? Am I any different than my brother and sister who aren't seen with respect and admiration? I am not! We are ALL children of the universe. It's the same way each of us are called to look at another, without the judgment of circumstances, personality, ethnicity, or gender. This idea of moving from our ego driven need to judge moves us away from our center of love that we are called to manifest within this world. This drive to hold each other and ourselves in contempt binds us from being the hands and feet of God, to one another, and ourselves.

Learning that truth within this relationship is something that I am still working towards. What I do realize is that it had to be something I would allow into my system to break down the illusion of the false self in order to see love. So when Eric told me he loved me, I believed him, because I had finally loved myself.

FORGIVENESS

"*THE HOLIEST OF ALL THE spots on earth is where an ancient hatred has become a present love*[14]." I simply love that quote. It is strong enough to stand on its own and no matter where any of us are our journey can begin to see how hatred can cloud a vision of love. We can see within the world how hatred of any kind stops us from looking at others in the world with kindness and hope. When we begin to see ourselves as enough and that we have enough, not abundance but enough, the greed of wanting more and being more settles into a love of self. When we experience that love, it quiets our individual egos and it begins to end the ideas that fuel our anger and need to be separate from others. It moves the perception of the very basic thing that we all do, that we are not all interconnected.

At the yoga studio I first saw the shirt, *Shift Happens*, I loved that play on words so much that we used it at our church, "With God, Shift Happens!" In our society we seem to be okay with saying, "Shit Happens," because we are quick to believe in the shit verses believing in the shift. Why? Because it's easier to gravitate to the negative. This idea, that it seems to be easier within our society to believe the negative things in the world, in people, in our jobs, in ourselves, in everything is based out of the tiny mad idea that we have bought into. It's evident in the way we hear about campaigns or even compliments about ourselves from another. But why can't we acknowledge the shift! Why can't we see that systems, world views, people, jobs, and ourselves are

---

[14] *ACIM - T-26. IX.6:1*

capable of change. That we are capable of opening our eyes and having *shift happen* that we never thought was possible. Each of our egos would love to have us believe that shift, or change is NOT possible. But isn't that ludicrous for us to believe?

On one hand we say, 'All things are possible for those who believe'[15] But then we grab and hold on tight with the other hand, *you can't teach an old dog new tricks.* It's an oxymoron and a trick of the ego that has been going on since the beginning of time. We say, 'God so loved the world...'[16] but then say, *this world is going to hell in a hand basket,* Which is it? If God loves this world, why would he let it go anywhere but keep all that inhabit this world safe in his arms. Does that mean crazy and really messed shit is not going to happen? NO! It means that we know we have a God, we are the inheritors of this love of God, and nothing can really pluck us out of the safety that is God. Because of that truth we can operate in forgiveness versus being vengeful and unforgiving. It means, we can move in the miracle of healing and love versus the dis-ease this ego said we should be in, un-love.

Eric and I don't keep our television on all year around. We turn on the cable when it's football season because we love a great football game. But one of the reasons that we don't keep the television on all year is because of what ends up being on the news. Hidden in the media, or even on the television shows, is hate, a little more hate, judgment, separation, or "better than other" mentalities. These moments fuel the illusion that we are separated from each other and we can talk and treat each other terribly instead of seeing each other as God's beloved or Christ manifested in this place.

Let me speak a little about the term, *Christ.* Because I want to move it out of the derogatory and anti-Christ way in which the Christian church has made it to be. The term Christ simply

---

[15] Mark 9:23
[16] John 3:16

means, messiah, or anointed one, and it pointed to the office and the function of the the person. So when we say in the church, Jesus Christ, and add Christ as if it is his last name and not as the function in which he came we are not speaking into how it was originally meant. With that understanding, why couldn't we operate in our Christ-ness? Why couldn't we operate in our function of being forgiving, compassionate, loving, full of grace and kind. Being the hands and feet of the one that is appointed to a certain act of service and function within this world.

Eventually, when I watch repeated messages of hateful banter of one group or another, I am going to manifest that in some way. But when I start to practice or listen to words of forgiveness and love, then I can begin to live out that truth. Shift Happens! It's funny I just realized that is probably the other reason I love Al Roker. Yes, you read that correctly. I love Al Roker. You see I have this, *love-thing*, for Al Roker and no one understands it. I guess I didn't understand it until this moment. He radiates a few qualities that only happen when you begin to shift from ego thinking to thinking that is lead by the Spirit. Non-judgment, joy, laughter, and love. Al Roker doesn't appear to be concerned with the ego in his commentary. He moves in his own skin in a very genuine way, you can tell he is comfortable with himself and the truth of his identity. That's critical in order to have shifts, to be comfortable with yourself, and with who you truly are, but first you have to find it and it starts with forgiveness.

A Time for Meditation:

We change things all the time. We change our hair. We change our clothes. We change how we say something. However, change may be the hardest activities for any of us to engage in. I think that we believe that change should be easy since we have to change so much on a given day. When a road is blocked off, we follow the detour and our route is changed. When a health scare happens, we change our eating habits or exercise routine. Change is inevitable.

So why is it so hard? Psychologists have discovered that there are seven steps to get to change. Awareness, Exploration, Commitment, Skill Development, Skill refinement, Internalization and then Change. That list is something we all go through whenever we change. Either it's a lightening quick decision or it's one that vacillates. But it does happen. They say the only real thing that we can count on, is that things change. In your meditation time today, allow some time to look at what needs to be changed in you. Perception, allowance, take risk or whatever it may be. But be kind to yourself, it takes time to change as you recite the lovingkindness meditation.

May I be happy
May I be well
May I be safe
May I be peaceful

Part 4

DREAMS AND EGO SCREAMS

S O THE DIFFICULTY WITH WRITING a book is that you have to be honest, completely honest, where it feels like you are laying completely naked before the world. Well, I guess you don't have to be completely honest but then what's the point.

If you lie to yourself your just keeping your own self boxed into the illusion. Like all of us, I don't like my shadow self but I believe it's important to acknowledge it. It's important to say exactly what it is we struggle with, and name the demons that seem to, "want their pound of flesh," like the song, "Shake It Out," by Florence + The Machine sings about.

So here are questions my ego has been screaming at me while writing: "What the fuck do you have to say about anything?! You are an in debt, ex-stripper, single mother, hustler, and you just figured out how to have a successful relationship."

Those ego rants have kept me stuck in all kinds of scenarios. From, avoiding my debt, judging my past choices, and undermining my ability to love and forgive. With that thinking I have always thought of myself as less than, and not seen myself as a child of the divine.

A huge lesson for me over the past few months is to know I am loved despite all of those ego moments trying to tell me that I am not loved or forgiven. Not only that I am loved, but also that ALL and everyone has that same love. No one person is better than another. The lies the ego screams, are the truths that the Spirit whispers. And that is the difficult part to hear.

You see, TO KNOW THAT WE CAN LOVE and ARE LOVED, and that everyone has the ability, is a huge lesson for all of us. We have to come to that truth. We have to come to the simple fact that it's all about love. It is love that helps me see my false attacks and judgment on others. Love helps me see only love. It helps me move past the projections that my ego would like me to live into, and because of all my ego screams that I have projected those areas of feeling inadequate in all types of situations.

When I was in college at Ohio Dominican University, I had a professor named, Sr. Miller. She recognized my "gift" and said to me, "Imani, you have the incredible ability to bullshit your way through the class. How about you use that great mind of yours and actually read the material?" I was taken aback. I had not experienced someone calling me out so directly, and in such a positive manner. I had been told, for years, that my ability to write had the limitation of a third grader. I had been told, I was not the prettiest girl around. I had been told, no one will ever want you, especially because you have two kids with two different fathers. All stories I believed in different ways that made me hold on to the ego tape that I was unlovable.

But ACIM says, "miracles honor you because you are lovable. They dispel illusions about yourself and perceive the light in you. They thus atone for your errors by freeing you from your nightmares. By releasing your mind from the imprisonment of your illusions, they restore your sanity[17]."

---

[17] T-1.I.33:1-4

LILY DALE

OVER THE PAST WEEKEND ERIC and I traveled to, Lily Dale Assembly, to see a workshop presenter for a book that we recently read. Things didn't turn out quite like we had hoped. The presenter cancelled. We planned part of our vacation around the fact that this presenter was going to be there, we had questions that we wanted answered based on his book.

In regards to Lily Dale, it's a spiritualist community that holds workshops on a range of topics and doesn't ascribe to a particular denomination, but is a religious community. There is a combination of lectures on reincarnation, past life regression, future life visioning, mediums, Native American rituals, Wiccan, healing, yoga, and a host of other topics. For us, we wanted to see a lecture that corresponded to a book that Eric and I had been reading, but wouldn't you know it, the author cancelled!

So, I was agitated to say the least. I had just finished camping over the past week. That was beautiful, well the weather wasn't, but it was wonderful being out in nature. I had spent time with new friends, and souls, that I felt like I've known for several lifetimes. I enjoyed a concert from, Bruce Hornsby, and Pat Matheny but I didn't stay in the beauty that I experienced, instead I focused on the lack. I wanted to ask the author questions and "do what I planned to do!"

My bubble had busted, my plans for how I saw my day going were changed and I didn't know what the rest of my time was going to look like. We walked the grounds while I held onto this huge chip on my shoulder. I was more than agitated as time went on. I was placing blame on the speakers and saying all kinds of things to myself about, "how could they," or, "what the hell?" I thought the end of our vacation was ruined, and so I stewed. I stewed so much, it was like people could smell a fire that was brimming off of me. And despite my wish to try and let it go, the inner conversation kept happening, so full of judgment. I could feel it creating a bit of tension between Eric and I, but not because of him, he seemed to be taking it all in stride even though he was also disappointed.

As a spiritualist community, Lily Dale has resident mediums who live on the grounds and, 'purportedly mediate communication between spirits of the dead and loving human beings.'[18] And so, after getting our money back from the main office we thought we would try this medium thing out, but as we walked around, we couldn't get into anyone! Not one person on the grounds was available, you can books appointments ahead of time and everyone was booked. Needless to say, I was on the verge of being livid and started blaming not only the speakers, but I was blaming Eric, myself, traffic, the ticket lady, the people that signed up for readings, the coffee lady, the whole universe! All because things didn't turn out quite like I'd hoped.

Eric very patiently walked with me through the grounds, we shared lunch, and talked about our intention for coming to Lily Dale. We talked about *things that connected us spiritually*, the premise of the book we read together, and why it had drawn the two of us to it, in very different times and ways. We split our very interesting jelly and turkey sandwich (something I would not recommend) and we looked throughout the program book they gave us at the entrance gate.

It was right there that Eric saw it first, and pointed it out to me. Susan Wisehart. Susan Wisehart was leading a workshop the same time that we were supposed to be in the workshop for the *other:*presenters.

---

[18] https://en.wikipedia.org/wiki/Mediumship

For those of you who do not know who she is, Wisehart deals with past life regression and soul work. She was trained by, Dr. Brian Weiss, who I guess, would be called the godfather of this work. She has been apart of Newton's work the author of, *Journey of Souls* (one of the first books of many that Eric purchased for me). There was an excitement that seemed to brim up, and I realized, well actually we both did, that maybe there was a reason things didn't turn out quite like we/I had hoped. So we stayed at the, White Inn, near town and we decided to go back the next day to see what would come up. And something did.

When I met Eric I had this rule. The 90-day rule. I employed this rule at different times in my dating life. Sometimes successful, sometimes not. Sometimes I viewed it as a suggestion more than as a rule, but this time I didn't want to do that. There was something about Eric that made me want it to be more. Now for those of you who don't know what the 90-day rule is; it's a dating technique I first heard about from Steve Harvey, a comic, writer, talk show host, and actor. His premise, was if an employer gives you a 90 day probation before you get all the benefits of the company, why then do women (or men I'm guessing) give up the prized gift of the (unfortunate name that Steve Harvey gave a woman vagina) cookie to just anyone. It needs to be earned.

I'm not saying this in order to make anyone feel guilt, project judgment, or even roll their eyes. It's just a basic premise I employed at times, and while it may be for some it may not be for others. I really think the main idea behind the 90 day rule is taking the time to get to know someone. A time to question. A time to listen. A time to learn. A time to grow. A time to heal. A time to explore gratitude. A time. I'm not going to say whether or not it was 90 days in perspective of the Steve Harvey principle, but I will say that it was a time of being very intentional with each other.

While I was at Lily Dale we eventually scheduled some time to see a medium. As a pastor within the Lutheran church, I can see that previous statement could be a bit shocking. I mean scripture, as we know it, talks pretty poorly about psychics, mediums, and astrology especially when it becomes something that replaces our trust in God. But I know that I was drawn there. I don't have problems with the idea of people connecting to the spirit world in many and varied ways.

So as I sat in with my medium there were a lot of areas discussed, and messages from my mother that were, quite honestly, spot on. One of the things that stood out was this idea from the medium of 90 days of writing. A 90-day rule for writing. It sparked memories my first 90 days with Eric and I and how it opened us both up. I knew the Spirit was leading me somewhere so I decided to take it on.

Before I start writing I pray, meditate, quiet myself, do a yoga pose or two, and then I ask for guidance. Eric seems to jump right into his routines, not without thought, but he can just sit down and start reading or writing. With that in mind, while Eric and I are both studying a book, he usually gets much further along than I do, quicker. You see, I'm a cross-reference kind of girl. I want to know where something came from, how it connects to another part, and even if it lines up with other aspects. So, I can be on one lesson forever, but that is not a bad thing and neither is the way he studies. It just is. And because of it I have found a gratitude to how we individually move. There is this lesson that says, "Love is the way I walk in gratitude. Gratitude is a lesson hard to learn for those who look upon the world amiss. The most that they can do is see themselves as better off than others. And they try to be content because another seems to suffer more than they. How pitiful and deprecating are such thoughts! For who has cause for thanks while others have less cause? And who could suffer less because he sees another suffer more? Your gratitude is due to

Him alone Who made all cause of sorrow disappear throughout the world[19]."

That lesson brings up, for me, the saying, "have an attitude for gratitude." Within that concept it removes the perception of judgment, that we are somehow better off than another. It ends comparison and brings us into unity that we share with all people, no matter where any of us are, because we are all in the same place. For that, we should give thanks for each and every living thing and see it as gift from the universe.

In my yoga practice, this is a constant lesson of non-judgment, to myself, or to others. You see, I was not always in the best of health. Two years ago, as I earlier mentioned, I was at my heaviest of 283 pounds, barely able to walk any distance or up a flight of steps without being out of breath. My joints screamed in pain. Today, as someone that didn't always care for her body, I can easily get into my head or my ego can easily get into my head, and I can hear all kinds of judgment. Not only to myself but to others around me. Things like, "well, I can at least do a downward dog, look at that poor lady over there," or, "look at that little bitty, I bet she never went through anything, bitch," or even, "I gotta do it harder and better because I'm a yoga teacher."

That inner dialogue with the ego moves me out of connection with the Divine. It makes me separate, better or worse, needy and afraid, or whatever other attributes you would like to add to it, but it moves me out of love. It moves me out of the connection we all have in God, that love we experience from God without judgement, and that we all deserve that love. When we walk in that gratitude we no longer see a divide between us all or even between worlds. When we walk in this way, there is no, poor lady, bitch, or yoga teacher for that matter.

You see, the interconnectedness that is here right now *is here right now.* We seem to compartmentalize the idea that we are body,

---

[19] ACIM - W-PI.195.1:1-7

spirit, good, bad, or whatever else, when the reality is that all we are is spirit, connected to each other and God. As soon as we can wake up from this idea that it's a we/them, us/they mentality we can have a better world in which we truly reside in. Having the attitude that we are all connected will truly 'pave the way to Him, and shorten our learning time by more than you could ever dream of.'[20]

---

[20] ACIM - W-PI.195.10.1

THE TOP TEN

Like a Quentin Torrentino movie, lets take this from the bottom to the top. Number Ten - "I get easily distracted." This is probably the easiest to identify with because we can all get distracted from time to time or in my case, moment to moment. But the others, I would like to explore a little.

Number 9 is this idea that *there is no such thing as coincidence.* While on our trip to Lilydale two very different people, recommended a book to me, that had never met me before. The book is, *The Game of Life and How to Play It*, by Florence Scovel Shinn, which was first published in the 1920's.

The first woman who recommended it to me was a vintage clothing shop owner, and professor of music at a local university, in a town we had visited. She helped me with clothing and turned on reggae as we shopped. She was delightful. The second woman was the medium I visited the next day. Her exact words were, "I don't usually recommend books but I feel like I need to with this one."

The principle that most people seem to grasp on to with regards to this book is success. Success is something that we all want in this world. Success, for many of us, is defined by the right house, job, car, and spouse with two kids and a dog. In the book, Shinn lays out the initial principles of success and what it looks like, and it's what some people may call a part of the prosperity classics. The back of the book even says, 'to understand the spiritual guidelines that will give them the framework to build a life of wealth and happiness.'

Now you have to know prosperity messages typically put me

off. It is not how I preach, the way I live my life, or even how I teach my yoga classes. Because prosperity messages simply mean, *I want it and I will get it, sometimes at all costs, even when it means myself and others may suffer.* Many times those that have preached prosperity, in my eyes, have been those that trick or manipulate people out of their money or make the average person, who may not have two pennies to rub together, feel like crap.

Laying aside that judgment I bought the $6 book and began reading it. To my surprise, the author opens up with an idea that always seems to resonate with me. The game of life cannot be played without a knowledge of spiritual laws. For some that may seem archaic but the reality is, we are arrogant to think that we started this, that we have all the answers just because we have certain technological advances.

The first principle that she starts off with is '*whatsoever a man soweth that shall he also reap.*' This means that whatever man sends out in word or deed, will return to him; what he gives, he will receive.'[21] From love and hate and all that is in between, this is a universal law. Even think of it on a very basic level of how the earth yields food. If you plant garbage with contaminated earth, your food supply will be contaminated. So why do we think that we can put words and strong energies out there that are negative and not see that return to us? As a saying goes, "where your thoughts go, your energy flows!"

I'm not saying it's a perfect formula because there are always times in which we wonder, "why is that person being nice to me, even when I was a jerk!" Or, "why is this person being a jerk to me, even when I was being so nice!" The fact is that we are free to respond to each other in so many different ways, but why not choose the sowing of love every time?

I'm reminded of the story in Matthew 13 where Jesus calls

---

[21] Scovell-Shinn, Florence. The Game of Life and How to Play It. Public Domain. 1928

Peter to come out and walk on the water during a terrible storm. The waves were crashing the boat and the disciples in the boat thought Jesus was a ghost. But Peter says to Jesus, 'if it's you, call me out to you.' And when Jesus does, Peter begins to walk on water but within moments he notices the rough waters and begins to sink. This passage is preached upon again and again, books have been written about it with the same principle, if you want to walk on water, you've got to take risks. The message's principle is simply this, take risks, keep your eyes on Jesus, and you won't sink!

However, quite honestly, there will be times that we will sink. The reality is there will be times when we will be overwhelmed by the waves. The reality is there will be times when we will take great risks and they won't turn out as we planned. What I think is important, in this text, is what Jesus does when Peter starts to sink, Jesus extends his hand and helps him out. If we believe that Jesus is perfect love or whatever way the universe operates, then why wouldn't he give perfect love in every moment, even in doubt. He understood the sow and reap of spiritual law. He would not have sowed criticism, harsh words, and least of all shame into this moment. He would have sowed love. So, I've begun to ask myself questions like:

- What if we sowed love today, even more in the midst of people's failures?
- How would the world in which we live be different?
- What if we sowed forgiveness, grace, and healing in every scenario?

The next area for me, is the grounding of yoga, or number eight in my top ten. I've been working on a program called, *Yoga 4 A Good Hood*, over the past few months. It has been an interesting journey. The basis of the program is that, I believe everyone should have access to a way to clear their minds, their space, and find ways to their healing. Typically in lower income neighborhoods or with people that are in constant crisis, due to poverty, violence, or just generational stuff, this seems unattainable. When I look around in my community I see a lot of people who are not breathing and I want to help them find breathing space. So I teach yoga to those who typically would not have access to it. Or wouldn't access it.

Because yoga has become the cool thing to do, in many ways it has also become something that isn't within the financial reach for so many. No matter what your socio-economic background, it just isn't something that you can go to. If its a choice of working more hours to help with bills, struggling to find your next meal, homelessness, addiction, or a plethora of other things - making time to quiet the mind is something that typically isn't on the top of the to do list. I just so happen to be blessed enough to practice in many different venues that I consider home, but that is not everyones story.

I saw a t-shirt at a yoga studio that said, 'No yoga, No peace. Know yoga, Know peace.' There have been several variations of that saying. Whether it's on meditation, prayer, God, Zen, whatever. There is something, about not having time to quiet the mind, that usually results in the truth that there is no peace that will be had. So, I offer yoga to those who feel that peace is nowhere to be found.

Eric said to me the other day, "you know that your main purpose in life is not to teach yoga." That gave me pause. I've been working so hard to teach yoga, become certified, and find other ways to grow my practice. I ran that statement through my head several times trying not to be offended, hurt, or even put off about it. Then I realized what he was saying and I absolutely agree with him. But what I said then was this, "Yes, you're right. My primary purpose is not to teach yoga, but to teach something that I learned from yoga; That my inner dialogue is not me, that

I am connected to the divine and the world, and so is each person that we encounter." The reason why I want to work with addicts, persons in recovery, victims of violence, perpetrators of violence, police officers, detention center workers, women, men, children, the poor in spirit in the pocket, the rich, the beautiful, and ones struggling with food on all kinds of levels is because there is something that I have realized. We are not our story. We are not what that inner dialogue has said to us. The voice that wants to keep us in the same place over and over again. Yoga helps with that and if that is the gateway to help people see that this game of our ego, that keeps playing with us, is not real then I will use it to get close and tell the truth of who and what we are. We are divine. We are love. We are forgiveness. We are healing. We are grace. We are grounded.

My mother is the most giving person I've ever known. In her mental illness and times when she was clear, it was her nature to just be a person of giving.

I remember when I was in Sunday school and I was kicked out because of my struggle of who God was as three persons and my mother as a schizophrenic. From conversations of God as fully human and fully divine or the Trinitarian concept, it was something that confused me. This was not a theological argument for me but rather just trying to understand it. During that time my mother was diagnosed and was journeying with schizophrenia and I asked a very simple question to the Sunday school teacher, "so, what you're saying is, God is schizophrenic?" I was immediately tossed out on my ear and not allowed back into class for several weeks. I was in high school and saw the reality of my mother's illness and how it was creating difficult moments for her. However, I still saw her generosity.

I am the youngest of four children and I've always only known my mother ill. My siblings had seen her well and then ill and so they knew my mother on both sides of the fence. Me, however,

I just saw my mother that was ill and it was always good for me. She made me laugh, she made me beautiful clothes, drew pictures, had the best handwriting, and always found a way to give me a gift. Now sometimes the gifts, I have to admit, were a bit odd for a young girl. There are two that stand out. The first was a pair of panties, from Mr. Lee's clothing store, that had a zipper on them. I was not sure at the time what the zipper was for but she thought they were pretty cool, and the 9 year old me should have them.

The other gift was one that I wish I had cherished a little more. She once made me a doll. She had little to no money and she wanted to give me something. So she cut off her hair, from her beautiful head of long black hair that I loved to brush, and stuffed it into panty hose and used rubber bands to make the limbs. At the time it was kind of creepy and I refused to play with it. I think this hurt my mother deeply, but in hindsight, I see the beauty of it. It was a piece of her, literally, that she creatively thought to give to me.

So, it would be natural for a teenager to reference God as a schizophrenic because that is what you have seen in your mother for years. It wasn't a slap against God, it was a valid point of trying to conceive this idea that God is three in one? Today I understand that much of our understanding of God will never be something that any of us will comprehend, truly. What I know is true in how we understand God is in regards to generosity, in how many persons there are; God cannot be anything that is against God's own nature. In my mother's illness, even though she struggled with many things, her core was giving and she lived that out. She was not selfish or self absorbed but rather fully giving because that was her nature. Mom, like God, like the universe, like the divine, like each of us is full of generorisity and grace and when we operate outside of that we fall in onto ourselves.

Number six is one that I go back to again and again. Kids truly do say the *darndest* things and they are usually the most truthful! One night, we decided to have a campfire in our backyard. As the embers front the flames floated up into the sky, I had to believe the smoke was like sweet incense into the nose of God because within the conversations seemed to be many prayers reminiscent of Revelation 8:4. Gary, Kira, Eric, and I, four friends, sat around the fire with Gary and Kira's two naked little babies playing their air guitar, singing AC/DC's Back in Black. We laughed and discussed different topics. It looked a little like this:

- "Wow, this beer may be better than KBS because it's not as overpowering, I can't believe I'm saying this!"
- "What's your favorite line in Frozen?"
- "Man, I can't do those fried foods back to back any longer! It sucks getting old."
- "Is this his 4th marriage?"
- "I want to keep my kids innocent."
- "I am no different than a rapist, terrorist, murderer."

This interweaving of conversations made some interesting transitions and pointed to the simple truth of innocence. The idea of innocence fascinates me, as well as I'm sure many others. Innocence is something we all wish we could get back to many times. But with the media it seems that innocence gets taken pretty quickly. As we talked about how we grew up and how we used descriptor words to identify people, Gary made an observation. Here's the conversation:

"I remember growing up and trying to describe a group of kids and there was one black kid in the group. Where we grew up, there weren't very many African American kids and so it was different. So, when I would try to talk about him, I would say, 'you know the black kid.' But with Ellison (his son) he was trying to point out one of his friends on his soccer team during practice, who was black, and then Ellison said, 'you know dad, the one with the orange shirt.' He didn't see his race but rather something to him that made his friend stand out, his clothes. I want to keep my kids innocent like that, man!"

As their new Aunt Imani, it was fascinating to me how they adjusted to me. They touched my hair because it felt different and they rubbed my skin a lot. It was delightful to have them ask me questions about my hair as they tried to get used to the idea. They quickly did and I was in love with these two boys, with their entire family. This innocence correlates with the other statement that Eric said to his friend, "I am no different than a rapist, terrorist or murderer."

In this moment you are probably asking yourself, "where is she going with this?" The idea that we are all innocent is a fascinating concept to me because it is very childlike and pure. To see one another as equal, sinless, and blameless is a radical thought. But let me be clear, I'm not suggesting that we are not to utilize the justice system that we have in place for those that have participated in heinous acts but as my grandmother used to say, "if it was not for the grace of God, that could be me." But rather, it is that we thought we could be separate from our source and each other. Our separating each other in these little groups based on race, gender, class, socio-economics, age, background, or whatever is a way for us to say or feel superior to another person.

In Galatians 3:28 it says, ' There is no longer Jew or Greek, there is no longer slave or free, there is no longer male and female; for all of you are one in Christ Jesus.' What if we saw the oneness again? What if we returned to the memory of God's love for everyone, no matter what they have done, who they are, what they look like, or how the act? When we begin to do that, more and more, then the innocence returns to us, much like a child. If we stop holding judgement against each other and begin to see those who commit, whatever injustice against another, and we ask ourselves, "what must have happened to this little boy or girl that drove them to this?" Can we then begin to offer them a reflection of who they truly are. Unchanged, unalterable just like they have been created. Or as it says, "You are and will forever be exactly as you were created. Light and joy and peace abide in you because God put them there.[22]"

What if we repeated to ourselves that lesson alone? What if we understood that yes, we will make mistakes but we are still unchanged just as we have been created. Perfectly. We would rather believe our mistakes or darkness and even our horror way before we believe the love, the joy and the delight. However, kids see it. They see it in each other, in themselves. They think they are awesome! It's so pure and holy. Wouldn't it be wonderful if we could do the same?

These messages formed my ideas of what home should be like, what I should be like, and what was acceptable and not. And because I couldn't fulfill certain things that I was supposed to do, prescribed to me by my ego, I found myself in a hole of debt, despair, and depression. I believed that to be my truth. But it wasn't, not only for me but for us all. The truth of each of us is unchanged, that we are whole and loved.

This brings me to number five in this top ten list. I own too much shit and too much shit owns me. And because it felt like I had to be defined by what I had, I stayed in that cycle. And because I felt like I could never get out of it, it dug me deeper into an even more vicious cycle. So I bought more, ate more, had meaningless and unsatisfying sex more. I just had to have more, more, and a little bit more.

In 2011, when I went to the doctor, he said, "Imani, you are at 175% chance of dying." My mind raced at that comment. My inner dialogue became the following words: 175%! What the fuck do you mean I have 175% chance of dying, you mean to tell me I have the chance of almost dying two times as much as the average person because we are all going to die! As he continued to comment on my declining health, and ways that my body was

---

[22] ACIM - W.PI.93.7:1-7

failing me, I realized the home that I called my body was letting me down because it was overwhelmed with the stuff I had put into and on it. I was 283 pounds, needed diabetes medication, suffered sleep apnea, had joint problems, and my heart was having difficulty working. My physical body, as my foundation, was cracked in my home and it was collapsing in.

Then, I went home, sat on my couch and looked at all the stuff I had acquired in my life. The things I thought I could never let go of. I looked at each item that I had acquired and realized the lie that became associated with it. I looked at myself in the mirror on my dresser and realized the distorted view that I had, even of myself. I thought about the reasons I packed on the weight and why I didn't see it or want to see it. I told myself I was too busy with work and my kids to want a different life for myself.

The next day, I had a meeting with a colleague. He and I drove together to our meeting in Buffalo and I told him about the conversation with my doctor and how he said, the best option for me would be to have gastric bypass surgery. I told him that I didn't have time to take off from work to do this because there was just so much stuff that needed to be done. He looked at me and said, "Imani, if you don't take the time, you won't have any time."

The following week I started the process for surgery. It took someone outside of myself to speak the words that I was afraid to say. It took someone outside of myself to see that I was not my work, my body, my stuff, or any of the things that I had placed on myself and that I needed to remember my true self.

Over the next 6 months I began a purging of the food in my fridge, of how I ate, items in my home and office, and tried to move forward with the commitment to have the surgery. Finally the day came, September 13, 2012, my daughter's birthday, I had surgery.

Today, by choosing differently, lots of things in my life are lighter. I own just a half a closet of clothes, only in the size I am. I only have one bookshelf of books (at home). I only have current mail. I don't own any extra furnishings, although I am looking to create my mediation room. I weigh 141.5 pounds. This purging of things that were not necessary in my life and realizing that I don't need to fill my life with stuff as if there was no stopping has changed and challenges me.

All the stuff in the world cannot make you happy. It never does. Eating the best meal in the world doesn't make you happy. Having a grand home, new car, a whole bunch of stuff, and even tons of money in the bank doesn't make you happy, because in an instant a doctor can tell you that you are at 175% chance of dying. The homes that we have made for ourselves in this life, although filled with family and the ones that you love are important and beautiful, the real home that all of us truly wish for is to be home with God. The reason we are wrestling in this life with all the items that we accumulate, is because we have forgotten that connection with the divine and we try to fill up with everything else. Sometimes I still forget it, but I'm trying not to. Though I can't remember where I first saw it, in my datebook and in the opening of one of my books that I read, now daily, it says, 'Each day for a least a few moments, think about God and how much you love him.'

You see, that's where home is. That's where our true comfort lies. They say, home is where the heart is. Well, our true love and true heart is with God, we just forget it sometimes because it's buried under so much stuff.

Well number four seems to be a resurgence of a topic in my life. I had these words written on a sticky note for years in my bedroom.

No More Tricks

These three small words guided me through my day. They were the first words I saw when I woke up and the last before I laid my head down. These three small words helped me through the most difficult times of my life as well as encouraged me through some nonsensical behaviors of my own.

There are several tricks that the ego will play on us. It loves to play on our guilt and fear, and they become the tricks that set us up. These tricks, are the friends of our ego, and they will tell us all kinds of things. They will have us deny or attack others and namely ourselves.

Eric said to me in the car the other day, "you are not what you think." Initially it can be an easy mantra to adapt but there are so many layers to that simple statement.

"You are not what you think."

None of us are, "what we think," but our egos would like for us to believe that we are. I read these words recently in *ACIM*, 'The ego vacillates between suspiciousness and viciousness[23].' Because of the fears and guilt that we latch onto we begin to sway back and forth between the judgment of others and self. We sway back and forth between hatred, loathing, and simply just being stuck. Again within and towards others.

I was recently interviewed by, Post Magazine, of Rochester, NY and I was filled with trepidation, joy, dismay, excitement, and even some, "what the hell, why?" All responses of the ego because it, *vacillates between suspiciousness and viciousness*. And the trick of my ego was to get me caught up in my individual self; not for the good of what it was for.

I have come to understand that my inner dialogue hopes I don't remember that this journey in life is not for me. Again and again, I typically forget that we are on this journey for more than selfish gain and I create these little or big evil moments of selfish bubbles. I wonder, how many evils have I created because I have been caught up in the tricks of my own mind. Of my own

---

[23] ACIM - T-9.VIII.2:7

ego. There was a beautiful article written about a snapshot of my journey into yoga and the project, Yoga 4 A Good Hood, I was hit in the face with my ego.

- "Who the hell do you think you are?"
- "You have not created a program as wonderful as she made it sound... you know there is some information in there that is not quite accurate, you're going to look like a fraud."
- "Your eyes are crooked!"
- "What is he going to think, what are they all going to think?"
- "You don't know these people you are trying to help!"
- "You're always going to be seen as a poor, overweight, single mother!"
- "Look, the church wasn't mentioned, you're going to be in hot shit!"
- "Um, people donated all kinds of stuff to the program, why didn't you mention that, loser!"

Those ego tapes began to scream in my head so loudly that I could not enjoy the present moment. I grabbed a drink of wine, laid down, and started down a path of panic!

Then I breathed and said those three little words.

No more tricks.

Whether it is writing this book, creating a yoga space that is accessible for all people, or just being fully present - I have to remember the words... *no more tricks.*

In all of our lives there are those moments where we are so wrenched with fear and guilt that we stop breathing. We hold our breath, brace ourselves for the worse and freeze. I see it all the time in yoga postures when someone is unsure or fearful of trying something new, they stop breathing. Then I say to them something to the effect, "Breathe. Because with each breath we can get into poses a little deeper, hold them a little longer, or just simply accept what is and what is not."

It's time for no more tricks and to let the ego fade away and see who you truly are. Beautiful spirit! For me, that *no more tricks* sticky note is replaced... with these words. *"note to self, just breathe."*

Witnessing to the truth falls at the top three spot of revelation when I was writing over the 90 days. It was about the 84th day of continued writing that I started thinking about this. It was a Friday and as I watched the local news I remember saying, "I don't ever want to be a witness to a crime." I say that with all sincerity, I just don't, period. Not only because I don't want to see a crime being perpetrated on someone but also because I don't always trust what I see. You've seen those specials on major networks where they test unknowing folks on the street and ask them, "what is it that you saw?" And always, they get it wrong. What they believe they saw, was not what it was. Something in their filter caused them to see or experience something that was not true. They see the "perp" of the crime wearing a blue shirt with green pants when in actuality they had on a stripped orange shirt with blue jeans. The information that they took in, was their truth, but it wasn't the whole truth. And that is where we get the saying, "there are always three sides to a story."

So what should we consider about the idea of a witnesses. A witness is a person who can testify to what he or she has experienced or knows first hand, right? In a court of law, the witness is not the defense lawyer. They don't have to explain why something happened. And the witness is not the prosecuting lawyer either, meaning they don't have to convince people to make a decision.

In that witnessing, it made me think about three characteristics of being a witness.

1. A witness decides not to worry
2. A witness decides to stand firm
3. A witness decides to live a radically different lifestyle.

Lot's of people in life have to enter into witness protection because of what they see and have to testify to. Their protection is so that they don't have to worry about what they are going to say or what others will think about them. For example, one of the things I have discovered in my yoga practice is that those three points are valuable lessons that we can hold on to on our mat. I don't have to worry about what my practice looks like. I can stand firm and I can choose to live a life radically different. My mat, is my witness protection location. It is my safe haven.

However many of us filter and play around with what we will bear witness to, because of what is in our heads and minds, and we think the "other" will not accept us if we witness to them something that we experienced. We want to then pull back our witness and protect ourselves so that we don't loose face somehow. We see that on our yoga mats also, we push ourselves, knowing full well we want to take child's pose and rest but we don't because of some story we have created in our heads about how we will be seen.

How can we practice our yoga on and off the mat if we are worrying so much? Worrying about who is going to judge us in the pose that we choose? Or how we will be perceived after we became vulnerable, took a chance, and then fell on our butts?

Too often we are afraid of making a fool of ourselves and so we don't trust our witness, to the roommate in our head, and thus don't trust ourselves. Then when we worry, we are stifled and we wallow in this unbelief and lack of faith in ourselves and our witness.

Yoga calls us to be free and not paralyzed by that worry and fear - AND instead we can do the following :

AS A WITNESS WE CAN DECIDE TO STAND FIRM!

When I hear the voice in my head (well that sounds a little crazy), that has become my bedfellow, that is my ego; my job as a witness is not to run and hide from it. Instead I need to sit with it and notice it. Instead, I must make a choice when I decide to be a witness, that everything I need is inside of me. AND, we have to trust the truest self, and like it says in scripture 'by standing firm, you will gain life.'

It's easy to stand firm when you got a pose that you think you rocked out. It's easy to stand firm when you are sure you're "right." But, it's not easy to stand firm when your toes want to point opposite of true north. It's not easy to stand firm in difficult poses where you have to press and rebound on one leg and your hips are fighting you. It's not easy to stand firm in the midst of friends and those that you love when you know they are not operating in their best selves. It's not easy to take what we learn on our mats and stand firm there AND when we are off our mats.

For me today, I started asking myself these questions about standing firm: *When am I as a yogi going to truly stand firm in the witness of my truth?* While simultaneously asking: *When does my standing firm and witnessing of my truth need to be silent?*

However, the principle of "do no harm" or ahimsa is real; do no harm to self or others happens, when I take the witness seat to my roommate and ask the question, what do I do with what I see? Do I do anything? Or do I just notice? Notice what is going on? Inside of me and inside of the other? And in the silence stand firm, knowing that I may not ever have to acknowledge something in the traditional ways. Maybe the witness just sees and records the data.

The third issue that I see in being a witness is deciding to live a radically different lifestyle once you become a witness. When we see something in ourselves, in others, in the world – when we are witnesses to that, how are we then going to react? Today, I was being kicked in the butt by the, "tap downs," that we had to do in our practice. I looked over at those who got down lower, knowing full well that I need to keep my eyes on my mat. But instead the roommate in my head started talking all kinds of smack about how inadequate I am.

In that moment, I just witnessed it. Well, first I beat myself up a little bit, but then I witnessed it... I didn't take it as the gospel truth. I just noticed what it was saying and realized it was not a truth for me. Now, on the other side, I did what I would call a great triangle pose and rocked it out and my roommate said great job, and instead of owning that also, I realized that was not truth either for me. The truth in that moment was that I was not present. The truth was I had stopped breathing. The truth was, I am a work in progress.

You see yoga is not just nailing the poses but many times we don't want to hear that. Instead of getting the poses correct, we should be focused on breath and what is going on in the mind first, and hopefully silencing the mind.

And I didn't feel bad or good about any of that. Instead, this time, I just witnessed it. I stopped worrying (even if it was just for a moment) and I decided to stand firm (even when I fell over) and instead of beating myself up for the rest of the practice I remembered something that Abby, one of our instructors, said about assisting:

- Observe
- Listen
- Give Tools

I don't have this witnessing thing down pat, but I'm trying to remember to observe my voices, listen to them, and try to figure out where they have originated so that I don't spew my stuff all over folks. My intent as a witness is never to cause ill for myself or others. But if we, or I, can figure this witness thing out, maybe then we can give tools that will help build up rather than rip down. Because that's not what any of want to do, right?

Discovery of our real selves is number two in my journey of realization. Many times we say that we are keeping a moment real when in actuality we don't even know our real selves let alone do we let another person see our real self. Because many times its scary to show our real selves.

That shit is scary.

Yes, I said shit... Showing our real selves means that we are exposing our tender underbellies and our inadequacies as well those places that we are most vulnerable. Other than the exhibitionist, I don't know to many people that like to be exposed or vulnerable. We don't want things that stink in their lives be seen. For me, I don't like exposing my real self to others but I know that I must. Because if my real self doesn't show up to the conversation, situation, relationship, yoga pose, whatever it may be - what's the use? However, I recognize the difficulty.

Remember I said, that shit is scary.

There is a quote from a children's book, that I find quite profound. In, *The Velveteen Rabbit*, by Margery Williams. It says:

"Real isn't how you are made,' said the Skin Horse. 'It's a thing that happens to you. When a child loves you for a long, long time, not just to play with, but REALLY loves you, then you become Real.'

'Does it hurt?' asked the Rabbit.

'Sometimes,' said the Skin Horse, for he was always truthful. 'When you are Real you don't mind being hurt.'

'Does it happen all at once, like being wound up,' he asked, 'or bit by bit?'

'It doesn't happen all at once,' said the Skin Horse. 'You

become. It takes a long time. That's why it doesn't happen often to people who break easily, or have sharp edges, or who have to be carefully kept. Generally, by the time you are Real, most of your hair has been loved off, and your eyes drop out and you get loose in the joints and very shabby. But these things don't matter at all, because once you are Real you can't be ugly, except to people who don't understand."

It's much like the issue of what is real in this world. Many times I watch people freak out about things that have little to no influence on what is real. If the truth is, *nothing real can be threatened,* then why do we respond to situations so negatively over issues that have no life giving power at all? For me, quite honestly, it's the fear that what we think is real, is not. WE doubt what is real, what has staying power, and that is how our ego survives and doesn't allow our true and real selves to show up.

Being honest and real about who we are and showing up REAL takes risks, and only people that get you will be okay with that real person, even if it's a little tattered and rough around the edges. Showing up real, heals. It not only heals those parts that may have been broken by folks that didn't deserve our space in the first place, but also it heals others around us. It gives others permission to be their REAL selves.

Imagine a world that is real. Where everyone shows their tender underbellies of vulnerability and we don't shoot them down or shame them for that but rather applaud them for being so courageous. Because that's what it takes, courage to face something that may be so unknown. I mean, we applaud men and women for going into the great unknown, so why not applaud and celebrate the exploration of the great unknown of our real selves.

Finally, number one is this idea of ForGIVEness. Dr. Martin Luther King Jr. says, 'Forgiveness is not an occasional act, it is a permanent attitude' or in *ACIM*, it says, 'It is your forgiveness that will bring the world of darkness to the light. It is your forgiveness that lets you recognize the light in which to see. Forgiveness is the demonstration that you are the light of the world. Through your forgiveness does the truth about yourself return to your memory.[24]

One night I was talking with my girlfriend of many years about the issue of forgiveness, the Spirit, and knowing the voice of God. She and I have been friends since both of our children (our oldest) were about 6 years old. We met in church, both single parents in college, and sang in the choir. In a normal circumstance, meaning if I was choosing my friends at that time, I wouldn't have reached out to her. She was an only child, seemed to be self absorbed, talked over people, loves math and science (and is quite honestly a whiz at it), and holds on to situations like a dog with a bone.

I've realized over our friendship, those traits that would normally have pushed me away, are areas in my life that I was resistant too but really needed to work through. You see, her only child behavior taught me about being alone at times, and loving it. My definition of her being self absorbed was really a lesson in teaching me about self care. Her talkative nature taught me to engage others. Her love of math and science, well that was a combo thing; it helped my children because I was utterly terrible at it past the third grade, and it taught me about the importance of being process oriented. And finally her stubbornness, it wasn't stubbornness at all. It was being grounded in her truth, and it taught me the art of debate and the knowing the when to be silent and just listen in a conversation.

One night when we where doing our normal gab sessions, I realized it was not one of those moments. She needed me to speak into her situation. Even though I was calling her because I was frustrated, exhausted, hungry, and wanting to get home to see the football game, she needed me to talk to her about the voice of God. So her opening question, "how do you know it's the voice

---

[24] ACIM - W-PI.62.1:1

of God and not just you?" The classic $10,000 question, right. I said the following,

"It's a relationship thing. You know when you were in a crowded group as a child and there were several children and several mothers. You may have been talking to your imaginary friend or your real friend in the midst of playing and suddenly you hear your name being called. There may be someone else with your name in the group and you may even be having an inner conversation, but you know that this voice calling you is one that is connected to you at a higher level. That my mother could be calling your name and you won't respond but when your mother does, well – you just do!"

She went on and talked about how she feels this urging to do something but she doesn't know if it's her own inner ego or God. I asked, "Is it something that protects the ego or is it rooted in a love and forgiving act?" She said, "Well, it's about survival not protection." I said, "Um, survival and protection are one and the same and that is always ego driven." As the conversation went on, she said, "Well, they offended me!" And then I responded with something I had learned from *ACIM*, my meditation time, Usually when we are offended by something or someone it is something that is in us that needs to be shifted.

For example, when another yogi comes in and talks with me about new yoga techniques, uses sanskrit, or discusses how a meditation practice has helped them, it doesn't offend me. She or he are fellow yogis and I identify with them. However, my underwear get into a bunch when someone approaches me about how to extend compassion to, "those people," of the world that, yes even I believe are opportunists and fear mongers. But the reality is, the "those people," *are our fellow brothers or sisters also. Heres the truth,* we are typically offended by what we perceive as opposite of ourselves. But the truth of the matter is, that rub that we are receiving, may be areas that we need to grow in while remembering that every attack you make, creates a weakness in self but for every time you forgive or choose a higher vibration of response you call upon your strength. Then, fear is removed with the guilt and pain and restoration happens.

For many of us, God may be more interested in changing our perspective than our circumstance. If we shift our perspective on a certain issue it changes how things look. When I said to my friend maybe the offense is an area that she needed to grow in, she paused and the debate was won!

Many times those offenses are areas in which the Christ in us wants us to learn. What if we began to look at things from God's perspective? Not the perspective that we have placed on God but the truth of who God is, from a perspective of love and forgiveness. I don't know if I ever noticed it before last night but the word forgiveness has two smaller words in it.

forGIVENess
forGIVEness

What if we realize what we have been GIVEN and GIVE it to others without question, without pause, and without judgment? You see that would kill the ego in our minds and the feeling that we need to protect something. It would slowly begin to kill the dream we have so wrapped ourselves into.

The final thing I said to my friend was this, "Do you know how when you first wake up from a bad dream, something wants to keep you there. You are hazy, you are trying to figure out where you are, even though it's your bedroom, it looks foreign." She said, "Yeah that's happened to me." I said, "Coming to a place of operating out of love and forgiveness is kinda like that, waking up slowly and shaking the cobwebs out of your head."

I read somewhere, and now I can't recall where, but it's on a sticky note, it says, 'forgiveness is a gentle remembrance of the truth we are one with God.' Operating out of the spirit to offer forgiveness to ourselves and others is a loving act. It destroys the inner dialogue, and it would be natural for our inner roommate to want to self protect and its not easy. But isn't it worth it to be free? And when we move our perspective from an ego centered mindset and realize that the Spirit in us is more interested in changing that than our circumstance.

And instead of Shit Happens ...Shift Happens! When that shift happens then we are lead with heart instead of ego. When that shift happens the questions move from "do I forgive or not? Is this right or wrong? Is this good or evil? Should I think of others or self?" But rather, how can I understand myself better?

There is a saying, "you can't ride two horses with one ass!" Too often thats what we do when living out this life. We can't say we want to open our heart and then close it at the same time. In regards, to the concepts of forgiveness and love, we have to understand that there are two higher frequencies to another person.

Forgiveness is a higher frequency of operating. Just like compassion, love and grace. Anything contrary to that, like revenge or hatred it just drags you down lower. For me, judgment becomes riddled with hatred and revenge, two things I know my ego would love to fall into, but I know that I don't want it to come to me, so why would I offer that to another person. Those lower frequencies freeze the heart.

Maybe this will sum up my top ten take aways this way. I like the movie Frozen. Yes, I watched that movie several times. Well there is a line when the king and queen take Anna to see the troll king because Elsa has struck her (accidentally, because Anna was a little too rambunctious) with her ice powers. The king says, 'You're lucky it wasn't the heart...the heart is not so easily changed but the head, it can be persuaded.'

SPECIALNESS

I HAVE ALWAYS WANTED THAT SPECIAL relationship. Growing up, I had the idea of being "special" in some way, waiting for that special person. Having a special love. I remembering watching "The Young and the Restless" with Nikki and Victor or "The Guiding Light" with Reva and Bud both soap operas that talked about special relationships and who was good or bad. No matter what either of these couples did individually or collectively their relationship was more special than and important. Every tabloid paper pointed out who was in or out. And I watched every Disney movie that made it clear that we are all looking for the special one! On top of that, while in high school we had the mantra, "I am special, I am (insert your name here)." I understand the importance to help with self-esteem that mantra offered. Mantras can be used to help people, especially young people. It gives a sense of self however many times it is at the expense of another person.

Now, that isn't to say that someone is not going to be special to you but its all about purpose or the content of how you see they are special to you. If it is rooted in a love that is healing or generous that relationship is sacred. But when the relationship shifts to just selfish gains, that's when it can become problematic. When our relationships become motivated by excluding others or manipulation, victimization and guilt all things that are counter to how the Spirit leads love stops flowing. And when love is not flowing we are not in alignment with how we are to live.

This is a point of struggle in my relationship with Eric but an area that I constantly meditate on. When asked about my love for

Eric I beam and I am excited about the connection that we share. Then I try to articulate that the same way I love him, forgive him, offer grace, and stand fully in his presence is the same way that I am called to do that with anyone I am with. The followup statement is, 'to say we have special love would be against what the Holy Spirit would want from any of us.' If we think something we acquire or someone we are with can make us feel love or whole then we are operating in special relationships and usually they end up manifesting themselves in our lives in a negative way.

When we realize that NO relationship is more special than another, we can realize that we are connected in God and called to love each other the same. If we practice the true purpose of love then we wouldn't make comparisons, fight about which political agenda is better, care about Angelina Jolie and Brad Pitt, differentiate between race, class, ethnicity, gender, or the other ways in which we attempt to place people in boxes. If we see each other truly as the identity in which they are created, as love, then we would respond appropriately - with love. Because like would recognize like.

A Time To Meditate

> Toe bone connected to the foot bone
> Foot bone connected to the heel bone
> Heel bone connected to the ankle bone
> Ankle bone connected to the shin bone
> Shin bone connected to the knee bone
> Knee bone connected to the thigh bone
> Thigh bone connected to the hip bone
> Hip bone connected to the back bone

...and it goes on and on. Perfectly connected. This body of ours is connected in a way that allows it to move with grace on a day to day basis. Now, that doesn't mean that the knees are in perfect shape or even the hips in my case, but they are glorious however they show up. Interconnectedness and awareness of how that shows up is important in coming to the conclusion that we are, as a people, one with each other. It would be foolish for me to stab myself in the foot because I don't like my toe nail color.

How many times do we do that in real life? Stab each other with unforgiveness and judgement. It is time to find ways in which we can see the beauty of "Dem Bones" that we are connected to so that maybe we can sing together.

In what ways can you see the interconnectedness in all people as you recite the lovingkindness meditation.

May they be happy
May they be well
May they be safe
May they be peaceful

Part 5

ONE YEAR LATER

NOVEMBER 19TH IS OUR FIRST date anniversary. Corny, I know. But it is yet another moment when I realized that I was on a journey of finding my true self and experiencing what true joy is. Meeting Eric in this lifetime has been one of the most eye opening experiences. Let me correct that, it has been soul opening. I correct that common used phrase of eye opening because many times what we see with our eyes is usually clouded by our egos, our judgments, and all the tiny mad ideas that we have created within this world. But there is something different with soul opening. It sees beyond whatever it is we have created because IT just IS and resides in the hand of God.

As a pastor, or even a yogi, it is expected that I am this genuinely loving and caring person for all of humanity. But let's be honest, it's a little crazy to think that. That should be who I live to be within this life. But, that isn't always the case. I typically see what I want to see in people. I typically judge what others do without any love in that judgment. If I'm honest, I judge myself in those moments that I'm judging others, which is a bit of insanity if you think about it.

For me, that first date was a moment in time, dare I say a *kairos* moment, which simply implies a God moment, when I realized I could no longer see with my eyes because they were so clouded. But rather begin to see with the soul and see that because we are in the hands of God, safe at home with God, the soul sees how God sees.

The true identity of our soul is joy. Our true selves are full of joy, and always trying to tell us something to pull us back into line.

- It has knowings.
- It urges us.
- It calls us to better selves.
- It moves us to great moments.
- It silences those arrogant thoughts
- It convicts us when we are being assholes
- It loves

I think that is why in great tragedy we see the better selves, or the better souls, of so many people. People just come together willing, to put aside all the stuff that they thought was important, and truly love complete strangers. They no longer see the person that they would typically be afraid of or cross the street to avoid contact, but rather they end up embracing that person and offering them safe haven.

That is what is so amazing for me about how we live this life I guess. That in such moments of devastation we forget what the eyes have seen, even though 99% of the time that is what we rely on, but in those moments, we cast all that aside and love with a divine quality. 1% of our true selves is trying to cry out to us and tell us to love this way all the time, but our crazy ego is trying to survive at all cost. The ego is trying to tell us:

- You know nothing
- Your urges mean nothing
- You don't have a better self
- Great moments only happen in the movies
- You're not arrogant but rather confident and the others are just haters.
- The world is filled with assholes so you're not wrong at all.
- Love is for suckers.

That is why this day marks such beauty for me. Remembering this first date with Eric is more than loving him, but rather realizing that within my soul is a calling to love others this same way. It helps me to see that there is something more than a superficial or 1% love in this life. This anniversary of sorts reminds me that I am safe in the arms of God and that I can listen carefully for how the Spirit is calling me to love more freely.

And that isn't crazy.

You see, I could've judged Eric based on his looks, that lovely blue shirt, or those "jacked" arms that were evident, or even his skin. But instead, from the very first conversation I wanted to lead with my soul with him and that was very different for me. I don't know why exactly I chose that with him, other than the fact that I had begun to do that with myself in my yoga practice. I decided to lead with my heart and not judge myself too harshly and hopefully, eventually, not at all. When I came across Eric I had started to see the beauty of how God sees me and all of humanity. So, that is an anniversary for sure worth remembering.

WHAT THE YAMA?

I RECEIVED A GRANT FROM OUR synod, our church governing
body, that allowed me to travel to India to study how the
ethical system of the Yama's and the Niyama's could influence
how we in the church lead. These ethical precepts essentially deal
with how and why we live both within this world and within
ourselves. These principles speak to how we should live out our
practice and are a part of the 8 limbs of yoga. The Yamas, the first
limb, deals with how we are to ethically live in the world with
integrity, while the second limb, Niyama, is all about how we
spiritually observe the world and discipline of the self.

They are as follows:

The Yamas
Ahimsa/ Non Violence
Satya/ Truthfulness
Asteya/ Nonstealing
Brahmacharya/ Nonexcess
Aparigraha/ Non Possessiveness

The Niyamas
Saucha/ Purity
Santosha/ Contentment
Tapas/ Self Discipline (fitness)
Svadhyaya/ Self Study
Ishvara Pranidhana/ Surrender

During my time in India, I focused on each of these principles for self evaluation and how they could be used for individuals, not only in the church, but as it could relate to getting back to who God has called each of us to be. At times I just went down the line of each of the yamas and niyamas, but there were moments when I was reminded of certain ones and just began to apply them to the situation, sandwiched between *Sutras*, Scripture, and sprinkled with *spiritual truths*.

The entire time asking myself, "Truth is truth right?" During the entire time however, I did practice Svadhyaya, or Self Study, which is embedded in the truth of, 'Nothing real can be threatened. Nothing real exists, Herein lies the peace of God.'

There are several things that I learned. One is the many things in our lives that we engage in can begin to undo ourselves from each other. The idea of ahimsa for example, the practice of nonviolence, manifests itself in the conversations that we have with ourselves about our self perception or the perception of another person. That type of negative self talk is violence to ourselves, and if not released from our ego will create a disconnect.

That is coupled quite accurately with Satya or truth. The truth of the matter is this walk, spiritually is not about seeking some superpower or reach some great fame or even an ascetic life. It is about looking inward at our own great teacher. Our own guru, which is self. You see between these two commitments within the sutras I have discovered, all that we need is within us.

I met two religious teachers in India. They wore there traditional orange garments, malas and seemed to smell of patchouli. They spoke with a gentle strength and assurance of living out this life. Swami Amrita and Swami Mukananda helped me with the principle of asteya, what that can mean for our lives, and how it all ties together with the other principles. Swami Amrita asked me, "How do we steal from God? How do we steal from each other? How do we steal from ourselves?" As she asked me these questions it made me think about the shopping habits of some of my travel mates and my aversion to it. During this trip full of delight and illumination there was one day when the shopping became out of control. It was eleven women going from vendor to vendor trying to get the best deal to stuff in their luggage at the end of the trip. From sari's, carvings, jewelry and statues it became overwhelming clear that we had began to steal from ourselves and no longer living in that moment.

So, I stopped. In that moment I decided to sit on a concrete stoop in the middle of a busy intersection in India and collect myself. As I sat there across from a Sandhu who was asking for alms and the aroma fresh chai being made I closed my eyes and heard the Ganges water crashing against the shoreline. As I sat in front of this local shop called, Scorpion, I breathed, drank a chai tea and had a bindi placed on my forehead by a local vendor that was walking around. Then something remarkable happened. Two dogs came and sat at my feet. At first I had a jolt of nervousness, but then I felt this overwhelming peace. I named one of them Gaya, I don't know why, I just did. Gaya became protective and would stand when anyone would try to come near me and sell me anything. So I closed my eyes and sat. By not shopping I had the opportunity to see what I steal ... the truth of who we all are - children of the divine and how many times I do not acknowledge that truth.

AFRAID OF THE DARK

I HAVE ALWAYS BEEN AFRAID OF the dark, and it is intensified when I'm alone. Whether it was the darkness that lurked in my closet, under my bed, or right outside of my house while I was inside. I qualify that statement by saying what was, outside of my house, because that is something that always confused me and even baffled my grandfather. I could play in the wide open spaces of the dark night outside without any fear. I would stay out and wander in the dark streets feeling safer than in my own home. But put in close quarters I look for my safety light.

Sometimes that still is truth for me. Granted, I don't like camping without a nightlight of some sort, yet overall I love the night sky and the beauty of the dark night. But, when I am home alone, I always look out of the window seeking to find what may be peering back at me. It's kind of ludicrous, I know, that I would worry about what is outside while I am safely in the house.

When Eric is traveling and I am alone, I always, and I do mean always, watch Robin Hood the cartoon from Disney. This children's movie provides me with the light that helps me drift away into sleep and forget about the darkness that surrounds me when I'm in the house alone.

I started thinking of this today because of the darkness that seemed to overtake me while I was struggling with yet another financial crisis. In the big scope of the world and within the structure of poverty that many people live in, I am way ahead of the curve, but because of circumstances that I have created for myself I seem to always be behind the eight-ball and find myself being knocked into the corner pocket. Even worse than being knocked into that pocket, I feel trapped in it, much like the house; and something ugly is peering back at me and I can't make out the figure and it scares me. So I would much rather be in the wide open space of the dark so that I could at least see what is approaching me from behind. So today, when my fears were coming from the inside, my Robin Hood was a bottle of Cabernet Sauvignon until I could drift into a calming sleep.

The problem with the Robin Hoods we tend to use is that the darkness is still there the next day and we have to figure out a way to deal with it. I am grateful that Netflix has the movie Robin Hood so that I can watch it online anytime I want, but I remember when I just had the VHS tape and it broke. Let's just say, I took me a long time to go to sleep. But the coping mechanism of using a video to lull me into the security of my childhood is not the way any of us should be trying to move through this life. The same is true for all the Robin Hoods of my life, whether it has been white or red wine, sex, religion (not to be confused with God), dancing on a pole or around one, food, or whatever it was that allowed me to escape the confines of my darkness.

I have been reading Pema Chodron's, *No Time To Lose*, and she says the following: 'How do any of us go from being completely self-absorbed in the dungeons of samsara to connecting with even a glimpse of longing and vast perspective of the bodhichitta?[25]' The meaning of bodhichitta is, 'noble or awakened heart,' which I am sure many of us are open to experiencing while trying to figure out how to be a person that is awakened. However, samsara is where we may have more difficulty, because looking at that is the only way to move towards the bodhichitta. I have heard samsara defined like this,

"the concept of samsara refers to the cycle of life, which includes birth, living, death, and returning to life. The term can

[25] Chodron, Pema. No Time to Loose: A Timely Guide to the Way of the Bodhisattva. Boston & London. Shambala Press. 2005. 25

be literally translated as continuous movement." It goes on to say, "the reason Samsara exists is that people fixate on themselves and their experiences. It comes from ignorance and it causes a state of suffering and dissatisfaction. Samsara in Buddhism can be overcome by following the Buddhist path to improving your karma."

So, what does all that mean, this Samsara? Well, for me, I translate that word to a small but powerful word... SCAR... The dungeons of scars could be a place that we all dwell in, and when we don't move from them we are never awakened into the true identity of the joy we are called to.

In one of my scared, to be in the house by myself moments about 23 years ago, I went to night club that was located on Cleveland Avenue in Columbus, Ohio. Instead of sitting at home, I found myself starting up my 1977, powder blue, Ford LTD and going to the club wearing a pair of overalls and a half top. Looking sexy, at the time, I pulled up to the bar and ordered a Long Island Ice Tea, at least three times. In the midst of that evening I see Will, a man that I had slept with in the past, just because, and Paul, a man that I had flirted with, who at the time I had no idea would become the father of my son. Paul moved towards me very strategically and let's just say, Will didn't like it. It was like I was a tree that he had just peed on, and I was stuck in this moment, while Paul began to grab for his member to show his was bigger. Within moments, bottles broke—one of them right over my head, by accident, allowing blood to flow over my face. In the next few moments, these two men fled from police, and an ambulance was taking me Riverside Hospital.

The scar that graces the right side of my forehead is a constant reminder of my fear of the dark. You see, when I was about 8 years old, a friend of my brothers would come over and begin the systematic molestation of my innocent psyche. He started out by coaxing me, just stroking my hair and telling me how cute I was. But it always happened after everyone was sleep. These dark

111

moments proved to me that the boogie man was real and his name was someone I knew, and close to our family. Over the two years of his overnight visits, it moved to more touching, and for years it gave me a very distorted view of men, sex, and ultimately what possibly could lurk in the dark. If I had faced my fear, of what had happened to me in the shadows, in a house, within this lifetime, then I would not have made the choice to go out that night. But as my grandfather used to say, "shoulda' woulda' coulda you can't change it, baby girl." So I can't change the past but I can change what is coming up by facing those things that scare me.

Now on a lesser scale, for example, debt is a huge fear for many people. Debt doesn't scare me, but my debts affecting other people scares me. When I say debt doesn't scare me I don't mean that in a cavalier way, because it does bother me deeply in some way otherwise I would have dealt with it earlier. Debt does overwhelm me, and I wonder how can I ever get out of it because there is so much of it, but I believe that God has abundance waiting for me, I just have misunderstood how that is to manifest itself over the years.

However, when my debt spills over to someone else it literally makes me want to crawl out of my skin. I worry about how others will then perceive me. In my ego, I begin to think that whoever the other is, they will then no longer love and accept me, and on top of that, the other, whoever they may be, will not extend forgiveness or even compassion. Which is absolutely the mad idea that my ego would want me to have.

Isn't that the truth of humankind. That is the reason Adam and Eve hid in the garden. Not because of their nakedness but out of fear that they had failed. After they made a mistake, according to the biblical story, they thought their failings would keep them from the love and forgiveness of God. So they covered up and hid. They operated in a manner that the ONE could manifest anything other than these attributes of love, foreignness, and compassion. They operated in a manner that God lacked these three attributes and decided to respond to that idea of lack, and not offer love, forgiveness, and compassion to each other and themselves - thus the cycle that we live in as humans. They are afraid of the dark.

But when we begin to operate in a spiritual existence there is never lack, there is enough love, forgiveness, and compassion for everyone, including ourselves. We won't need to find Robin Hoods to allow us to feel safe. If we truly believe that God is all-encompassing of these features then how can God have attributes of the negative. Where there is light, there can be no dark. So where there is love, there is no lack. Where there is forgiveness, there is no vengefulness. Where there is compassion, there is no lack because in love, no one can experience shortage.

There is a saying in the Lutheran church that I have stated several times, 'we are the hands and feet of God.' What does that mean? It means that we are to offer the same kind of love, forgiveness and compassion to the world and to ourselves that God does. When we are living how God is calling us, to love and be loved, extend forgiveness and compassion; we begin to invoke what cannot be erased... our true identity.

So, when the perceived darkness comes, even though there may be material lack in the moment, there are ways that invoke abundance of God. Simply by realizing who we truly are.

NOTHING REAL CAN BE THREATENED

"I CHOOSE THE JOY OF GOD instead of pain" and Pain is a wrong perspective. When it is experienced in any form, it is a proof of self-deception.[26]"

These words came at me with such force. It's like my tattoo artist Ferg says to me, "pain is just an illusion, Imani. It is just the skin sending messages to the brain that something different is happening." Well, this morning I felt as if I every nerve ending was being poked and prodded and all my pain from a lifetime came crashing down on me. I've avoided dealing with pain that I have experienced for years, hoping in the avoidance that it would just go away. It has been like not opening a utility bill, in hopes that if you don't look at it, it doesn't exist.

We, overall, are hiders. We don't tell the truth of how we really feel, how we hurt and even struggle. My grandmother used to say to me, when I had bad dreams, "baby girl, if you tell someone about those dreams, they will never come true! So it's ok to speak them, it will help keep the demons at bay." My avoidance of my demons, has always been a way of trying to ignore them fully but I am now having a better understanding of what has been going on inside of me. It has been the survival of the ego or the tapes that play constantly in my mind.

During this past year my dreams have become so vivid, especially the negative ones. The more I become at peace with one area and let my old nature float away, the louder my ego splashes around, as if it is drowning and trying desperately to

---

[26] ACIM - W- PI. 190.1-11

survive at all costs. As a woman that does not swim it is a powerful analogy for me. You see, whenever I have tried to learn how to swim it was like fighting the water, because of this fear that I was going to be consumed by it. It's even something that lifeguards learn about! It's hard to save a drowning person because they will drag you down to stay alive.

That has been the little monkey in my mind often times. It has been trying to survive at all costs. It has been fighting me to stay in a cycle that I no longer believe in. That inner roommate of mine has been kicking and screaming in the water afraid that I will continue to float on this barge of thoughts that was taking me nowhere good. Thoughts around:

- You will never be financially free.
- You cannot do my job well enough to move it forward.
- Eric will leave you.
- Illness will consume your body.
- You cannot write a book and you have nothing to say.

When those types of thoughts begin to have their own tape player in my mind they start to dictate everything else. For example, I was not honest with Eric that I had been having these thoughts, so I became anxious, clingy, and shitty. They moved me to the point of irrationality, and remember, *"pain is a sign illusions reign in place of truth"* or as my Aunts, Jwahir and Azuka, used to say, "fear is just False Evidence Appearing Real." Fear was guiding my feelings.

My aha within this time period was that my fear points to the truth that there is a light within me, and it is the same light within all of us. My fear is not about inadequacy but how I am called to serve the world. It's easy NOT to be of service. It's a challenge to us all, to know we are all worthy of love, forgiveness, wholeness, grace and so much more.

The practice of choosing joy is the practice of forgiveness. It goes hand in hand. Forgiving myself for choosing the script of pain that leads to thinking that I am, or anyone for that matter, is inadequate. I have shrunk in the midst of others to make them feel more comfortable. I have held my thoughts inside because of thinking it will be wrong. I have stopped myself from floating safely on the river of truth. I have chosen pain in many, and different, ways.

Recently I woke up asking myself, "Why not choose joy because I am not this body and free in God?" Choosing joy is the lifeguard that is trying to save us from drowning in the illusion, but the ego would have us flail our bodies around and drown everything and everyone around us, leaving us in choking on water.

There have been many attempts over the summer to learn how to swim, Eric has said the same thing over and over to me. "Imani, you don't have to fight the water just allow it to carry you and move your arms and legs with it." Relaxing into a moment has never been my story, I've always been a bit of a fighter or resister of things. I will fight for what I perceive is mine, what needs protecting or at times just because I think someone is being a jerk. But since I met Eric last year he has continuously said to me, "you don't have to fight." Which in turn makes me say, in a momma bear tone, "what do you mean I don't have to fight." But it is a truth that I think I'm starting to get. Because I want to choose only joy and forgiveness.

I have tried for years to be something that I am not. But once I realized the simple truth that, "nothing real can be threatened," I could begin to be free in that simple truth. This simple reality is seen in every piece of religious, philosophical, mathematical, and universal laws. It is a truth that happens on a yoga mat when ones gaze, breath and foundation line up. It releases us from judgment and moves us to love. Once that awareness happened, I could begin to lay down my judgement and walk into my holiness and even more so, see it in others.

A Time to Meditate

"When we begin to operate in a spiritual existence there is never lack, there is enough love, forgiveness and compassion for everyone, including ourselves." When I wrote those words it landed so strongly in my heart. It made me think of the time when we used to have "wish sandwiches" growing up. A wish sandwich was two pieces of white bread with mayonaisse, mustard or ketchup in the middle and you WISHED there was something in the middle. We resentfully ate our sandwiches in hopes that when we recieved our goveernment cheese or the bologna with the red rind on it that we would have then had all that we needed. In hindsight we did. We had food. It didn't look the way we thought it should but it was there. Eric didn't arrive in the package I thought he would and I'm pretty sure I wasn't either. But in us there is no lack. So it is true with all of us. There is enough love to go around because love never runs out, unlike a pack of bologna.

Take some time today in your lovingkindness meditation to send love to someone that feels as if they are unlovable. Even if it yourself.

May I/ You be happy
May I/ You be well
May I/ You be safe
May I/ You be peaceful

Part 6

SAY WHAT BILLY JOEL?

C AMPING IS ONE OF MY favorite things to do. I knew that Eric was someone that I would love to spend my life with when he talked with so much passion around camping. Finally, someone who got it! I had been invited to Las Vegas or Atlantic City for some fun at casinos, and yes that could be fun, but I love being outdoors and going for a great hike in a glen, or trail. So needless to say, I was having a great time one summer with Eric, and his friend, while we enjoyed a campfire and some tunes.

There are a few differences between Eric and I. He loves music, especially classical and can name an artist at the first note that he hears. I on the other hand enjoy classical but I could take jazz over it. He is a process thinker and I am a vision thinker. He is naturally athletic and I am a bit of a klutz. He loves the sun and doesn't burn, I can take the shade with hints of sun and burn like crazy. He is white, I am black. Even though the list seems to be a tool to point out the way society separates us, that is not my point. I don't usually see those areas of separation and most people wouldn't know them on the onset of seeing us either. Well, except the white/black part. At times however, I forget about our differences. I don't typically see the polarization of our society but rather gravitate to that which unifies us.

I don't know if it's Eric's military training but he is always watching and looking around. I think that's one of the reasons it makes him a good process thinker. Whether it's while we are hiking a glen, walking into a store, or camping, a person may not see it but he is always watching and processing. During one of our camping trips to Sugar Creek Glen where the legendary, Poags

121

Hill Motorcross Climb, is held, we had a bit of a conflict! Truth be told, I became outright angry with him. You see the PHMC draws a unique crowd. Nice enough folks, and overall very friendly, but let's just say you don't see very many people of color in this crowd, let alone interracial couples. As we where playing music through the camper, like so many, we listened to everything from Maroon 5, Justin Timberlake, Dixie Chicks, Carole King, Elbow, and Evanescence; notice a trend... all white artists. We were having a great time and great discussion about Justin Timberlake and how much Eric likes him, while our friend, Jonathon, commented that he is not the biggest fan. I said, "Oh, have you heard Justin on the Jay Z song, Holy Grail?" Well, not being the biggest rap fans both of them said, "No." I proceeded to play it, and then the rub happened.

Eric looked around and joked about offending the neighbors, blackness, rap, and "psycho bitches." I became livid, turned off the song and put on, "Honky Tonk Bodonkadonk," by Trace Adkins, and no one seemed to be offended by that. I walked off, hurt and pissed.

While I was trying to find the remote to the speaker and having a drink, I stewed, and Eric realized something was wrong. Jonathon joked, "the honeymoon's over dude," which only pissed me off more. As if I was one of the, "psycho bitches," that Jay Z rapped about. I told Eric when he came over why I was hurt and angry, and he just listened. It was simply that he looked mortified when I put the music on, and how does my blackness offend the surrounding folk? He apologized, and told me what he was thinking. He said the following,

"Imani, you don't offend me and I am so grateful to be with you. But everyone around here doesn't know you and they have some distinct feelings about what they think you represent. I don't want to start any shit here so I just didn't want that... that's all."

In that moment, I realized what Eric has been doing. Watching and thinking as he always does. He heard the music and "Duck

Dynasty" references and t-shirts of our back camping neighbors. He realized the closed mindedness, and how they would see themselves as separate and special, and that I was beneath and not so special. He was trying to protect us. Protect me. Then shortly after, Eric sang the words of "You're My Home, to me. Words like:

When you look into my eyes
And you see the crazy gypsy in my soul
It always comes as a surprise
When I feel my withered roots begin to grow
Well I never had a place
That I could call my very own
But that's all right my love
'Cause you're my home

One of my favorite scriptures is when Jesus said in John 14:1-3:

"Do not let your heart be troubled; believe in God, believe also in Me. In My Fathers house are many dwelling places; if it were not so, I would have told you; for I go to prepare a place for you. If I go and prepare a place for you, I will come again and receive you to Myself, that where I am there you may be also..."

I have read those words during funerals, sermons, counseling and even devotional times and they move me each time. Knowing I have a home in God gives me comfort and it's a reality I think we tend to forget. So the perceived or even "real" troubles we have in this life are nothing when we think of the truth that we have a home in God. Does that mean, the stuff of this life doesn't hurt? Absolutely not! My fight with Eric hurt my heart and his. Loving him as I do, why would I want that hurt to happen or continue.

A preacher, who I don't remember at this time, once talked about how we treat each other here on this big rock and he used this as an example. He said, "what if that person you hurt, avoid, or judge is in the arms of Jesus and the Christ is inviting you into those same arms? Would you still hurt, avoid or judge that person? Then why are you doing it here?"

I thought of this while I was sitting with Eric, in this camper, as I could see the pain in his eyes that was created by my ego nonsense. I would never want to create that kind of pain in anyone. The other person affected by my ego diarrhea was Jonathon. He tagged on his comments about Jay Z and it felt horrible, so I opened my mouth and let it spill out, like vomit, and it didn't have to. That same look was in his eyes. He was apologetic and he loves me. Now, he didn't sing, "You're My Home," like Eric but it was at that moment I remembered when hearing those stories preached along with what it says in in so many spiritual literature that we are not separate, that we are about love, that we are perfectly safe, and in ACIM that we are at home with God but capable of awakening to reality. We just to to reconcile the truths of love and when we do, in an instant we will see what is eternal and true.

My grandmother, when asked how she was doing, always use to say, "baby, I'm clothed and in my right mind." I didn't fully understand that statement back then. But in the Bible there is a story of the demonic he healed that were in the cemetery rattling his chains, naked, and tormenting folks, within just a few verses we see him "clothed and in his right mind" and healed by Jesus. The ego forces us out of our right mind and makes us think that we are not only separated from each other but also God. We attack each other, and God, on a daily basis because we believe this lie.

However, what if we trusted when the Holy Spirit says that we are loved and forgiven? That, "nothing separates us from the love of God," and we in a Holy Instant could be in right relationship and awakened to this truth. Maybe then the words of Billy Joel "You're My Home" would be more than a sappy song between two people that love each other but rather a song of love between us, God and all of creation.

THE BELL TRAIL

ERIC ASKED ME TO MARRY him on March 31, 2015 at an oasis at the end of Bell trail in Arizona. It was a shock for sure, because he actually caught me off guard. He went off to the back rocks as I was taking in some much needed sun and feeling full of bliss. When he came back he kneeled down before me and said, look what I found in the sand. I still was not clued in that he was on one knee and that in this rubble of rocks and beautiful Arizona red sand was a ring for me.

I said, "Oh my goodness, someone lost their ring!" He looked at me as if to say, "*Really Imani?*" And there was a gentle laugh in his eyes. Then I got it, and as he asked me to marry him, I felt a rush of spirit softly kissing me. I said yes one million times in a single breath, it seemed, but was speechless. I didn't realize I hadn't spoken my yes, because as a complete stranger on the trail noticed what was going on, shouted congratulations, Eric said, "well, I don't know if you should congratulate us, she hasn't said yes!" Then I said it loud and clear. "Yes, yes, yes!" A trinity of yeses, that matched how he always kisses me three times, and I was flooded with this gift of love.

As I have meditated on this extraordinary reality, I find myself agreeing with one of the most important things C.S. Lewis ever taught me. In his book, *The Four Loves*, Lewis looks at the Biblical concepts of love and then comes to the conclusion of the distinctions between Greek understanding of love: the difference between what he calls, need love, and gift love.

Need love, Lewis says, comes out of emptiness. It is intrusive at its root and when someone is operating out of it the one that is the lover sees everyone, and everything as something that they can possess. It is greedy and wishes to suck the life out of that which it wishes to hold in its grasp.

Now I know that many times, as preachers, we diagram love as a circle but I want to challenge that and it's something I heard in sermon once before. If we draw love as a circle it gives the impression that the person is in, "need," of that love and the person is incomplete in their creation, as if they have to have someone or something to fulfill their needs. And we are back to the need for special love. So, if we were to diagram it, need love as circular, that means the person is reaching out to another person in order to transfer value back to themselves. You see, need love is just needy. It is always concerned with just getting back to themselves. C.S. Lewis concludes that when we start talking about loving someone, basically, we are basically just saying I need or want you AND your value, because I desire to make you mine.

Now juxtaposed to that, Lewis contends that gift love does not come from a place of lack but rather from abundance or fullness. Gift love has only the purpose to enrich that which it loves and will never take away its value. So the image that I heard in a sermon was one of an arc, NOT a circle, because 'it moves out to bless and to increase rather to acquire or to diminish.' Lewis concludes this contrast by saying that the uniqueness of the biblical vision of reality is that God's love is gift love, not need love.

And then he says,

"The Gift-loves are natural images of Himself; proximities to Him by resemblance which are not necessarily and in all men proximities of approach. A devoted mother, a beneficent ruler or teacher, may give and give, continually exhibiting the likeness, without making the approach. The Need-loves, so far as I have been able to see, have no resemblance to the Love which God is. They are rather correlatives, opposites; not as evil is the opposite of good, of course, but as the form of the blanc-mange is an opposite to the form of the mould.[27]"

As I look down at the ring that he chose for me, I see these realities manifested. The once empty circle that was once greedy and needy is supported by two separate arches that have come together to relieve and fill it with true gift love. And that gift love is represented in a single piece of amber. Not a diamond like many have thought I should have, but amber because he remembered is my favorite, and not a gemstone as many mistake it for but a fossilized resin. I like it not only because of the color but because of it's many uses. For example, young amber is soft and used for purification rituals, that youthful amber is 1000 years or so old. But Amber is said to have healing principles much like the gift of love.

So as I look onto my finger, I am reminded and humbled, but mostly filled with love. Not only for Eric but on the Bell Trail I came to a conclusion that I wish to provide this same gift love to all. This act of love through Eric, from God, that is in each of us has been a push to write more, but more so, to teach about the gift of love, forgiveness and compassion for all of humankind.

My hope filled prayer is that we forgive what we think we have done to the world, our neighbor, or enemy, and even ourselves. That all of humanity sees the sins we believe we have committed are just projections of our guilt and that judgment is a secret sin that we need to be free from. Just like I believe that the Holy Spirit wishes for me to return to my true identity, which is still a work in progress. I believe that it is a call for all of us to return to our true selves and see that nothing has separated us from God's love.

---

[27] Lewis, C. S. (1971-09-29). The Four Loves (Harvest Book) (pp. 127-128). Houghton Mifflin Harcourt. Kindle Edition."

MY TRUE IDENTITY REVEALED

WHEN I WAS BORN, I was given the name Kimberly Elizabeth Dodley. My mother called me Kimmy until the day she died January 4, 2013. Growing up, some of my family started calling me Joy. I guess overall I have always been a goofy, happy and rather joy-filled child. I enjoyed being around my family and being home. Especially with my brother Mark, he is the one who primarily called me Joy, something that he periodically still does today.

However in my 20's my father started calling me another name. The name that I legally changed to several years later. Imani, which means faith. Now, even though I was an overall happy child I've always struggled with the understanding of God, Spirit and aspects of faith. I've always had a pull to understanding the Divine. I've studied what it would mean to be a Buddhist or Muslim, and spent some years in each of those houses. I've looked at what it means for me to commune with nature and how God created such beauty. There have been times when I've been so wrapped up in my thoughts of God, even when partying that I've felt an ecstatic rush of Spirit. I'm drawn to it.

I remember once we had a party when my father was out of town. There were at least 30 people in the house, there was some drinking, and pot was being passed around. I had a few drinks, but not much because I suddenly got nervous about the fact that I was having this party in my father's house and people just seemed to keep coming! In the midst of this party, I remember being drawn into the kitchen. I just wanted to escape all the noise, not much luck there, and just evaluate the situation. Without thinking, without having EVER done this, I felt what I can only describe as a gravitational pull on to my knees and I was on the floor praying. My girlfriend Patrice walked in and she was moved in the same way. Let's just say, the party didn't go on much longer after that. It was a glimpse of my true self.

The people that truly know me, know if someone tries to say something about me, whether or not it is true. Matthew 16:13-20 that says this:

"when Jesus came into the district of Caesarea Philippi, he asked his disciples, "Who do people say that the Son of Man is?" And they said, "Some say John the Baptist, but others Elijah, and still others Jeremiah or one of the prophets." He said to them, "But who do you say that I am?" Simon Peter answered, "You are the Messiah, the Son of the living God." And Jesus answered him, "Blessed are you, Simon son of Jonah! For flesh and blood has not revealed this to you, but my Father in heaven. And I tell you, you are Peter, and on this rock I will build my church, and the gates of Hades will not prevail against it. I will give you the keys of the kingdom of heaven, and whatever you bind on earth will be bound in heaven, and whatever you loose on earth will be loosed in heaven." he sternly ordered the disciples not to tell anyone that he was the Messiah."

Jesus, the Christ is asking who people say he is and the disciples, those closest to him are throwing out answers. They are saying what everyone else is saying. But they don't seem to really know. They throw out words but they don't have any true understanding of who Jesus, the Christ is. This idea of Christ is more than some add on name, or some last name of sorts, it's an energy that is released into the world that shapes the heart and the communities, one person at a time. Anyone can say my name is Imani and not know who I am. Anyone can say Jesus is the Christ but not know who the Christ is.

If we truly begin to think of Christ as forgiving, transforming, healing, loving, inspiring, full of grace, and kindness that energy would transform us and others. It is an energy that we all need but also are called to give. It is an energy beyond doctrine or a church. It is an energy that is within all of us. However, it is usually stifled by our ego and everything around us that says, we don't have to be that forgiving, transforming, healing, loving, inspiring, full of grace, kindness energy. In *ACIM*, with the section titled, The Branching of the Road, I particularly like the wording of the 4th paragraph that says,

"think of the loveliness that you will see, who walk with Him! And think how beautiful will you and your brother look to the other! How happy you will be to be together, after such a long and lonely journey where you walked alone. The gates of Heaven, open now for you, will you now open to the sorrowful. And none who looks upon the Christ in you but will rejoice. How beautiful the sight you saw beyond the veil, which you will bring to light the tired eyes of those as weary now as once you were. How thankful will they be to see you come among them, offering Christ's forgiveness to dispel their faith in sin.[28]"

I recall a beautiful conversation with Eric's mother Kathy and her friend Melody. We started talking about choosing what I like to call "our best selves." It's something that Kathy said that she has heard me say and has started using herself. As we had this conversation about neighbors that sue, racism, hatred against homosexuals and church acceptance on change, Melody chimed in about how she has not been a very religious person because of all that judgment in the church. I laughed and said, "Me too!" But then I said to her, "What if we all chose love instead, what a different world this would be. Look at Eric and me, years ago we wouldn't be together because of our obvious differences. But because I try now to see love only, we are together. Love of myself and love of him." She smiled and said, "you know my sister, who is from the deep south and very religious said the same thing to

---

[28] ACIM - T-22.4.4

me, all you need to do is love Mel." Then Kathy chimed in and said, "Yes, we need to just choose our best selves."

What a beautiful world this would be if we just did that - took what we know and what was true and let it shine. What if we just chose our best selves? What if we stopped working out of our fear but instead our power? What if we began to see and act like we are the enlightened children of light that are free to manifest that freedom to others.

Knowing that truth solves all of our problems. The real problem. The only problem that truly matters. This truth reminds us that we are all connected God and that we are not prisoners to the things of this world. This provides us with the truth that sets us free. Why not let, 'freedom come to make it's home with [us] you,' because that's what the woman with the 12 year hemorrhage did! She let the power of Christ's forgiveness free her by just reaching out to him, she just knew that Christ was the way, the truth and the light. In Romans 8, it says, 'there is no condemnation for those that are in Christ Jesus.' So, let's stop beating ourselves up and walk into the bigness that we are called to, letting our light shine so that all can be free. And when we do that, we will know our True Identity. That we are one with God and we are love.

NOT JUST MY IDENTITY,
YOURS, BUT OURS

"To perceive errors in anyone, and to react to
them as if they were real, is to make them real to
you.[29]" "When a brother behaves insanely, you
can heal him only by perceiving the sanity in
him.[30]"

For most of us, these two quotes will be difficult to reconcile
within this world today. It is especially hard to articulate these
quotes to members of my congregation, or anyone for that matter,
in a world with so much anxiety around violence, immigrants, or
anyone that is other. When I have watched the news in an attempt
to try to get a handle on the energy that seems to be sprouting up
in me, and in the people that I serve at my church, I seem to go
back to those two quotes. We as a people are anxious about the
end of times, the beheading of an American, the riots in Missouri,
or a fight on a plane because one person rigged the chair so the
other couldn't recline and they are blaming it all on other. Even
when there is a conflict in the church between two parties, it's
always "their fault."

We judge the Palestinians, Israelites, Africans, or whoever it
is that are fighting and say, "how crazy they are." We judge the
drug dealer, rapist, killer, the black guy, the white guy, the man,
the government official, the litterer, the addict, the victim, the

---

[29] T-9.III.6:7
[30] T-9.III.4:5

one who has been killed, and countless others and ascribe blame onto them. I love that the section in *ACIM*, The Correction of Error, is right after, The Answer to Prayer. Within that segment of answer to prayer there is a portion that talks about how the way we perceive our brother reflects onto how we pray. I mean, many times let's be honest, our prayers are more like, "fix them, fix that situation, make them stop," or something like that. We don't see our brother or sister and their "insanity" in a way in which God sees them. We don't, "love [them] for the truth in [them], as God does."

But instead, we think the way to correct an error is to beat someone over the head with our words, judgment, and fists to make them stop. But the truth of the matter is, we cannot. That is a journey they have to make, so why not just see the simple truth in them, that we are all loved.

All of us, at some point, wrestle with feelings of inadequacy or feeling loved. Many, like myself, struggle with the anxiousness, that the ego brings up, about how people will judge those inadequacies. The truth of the matter is, I know I will fail in sometimes and not get it quite right. In some ways I am okay with it, but because I know that some people will not be okay with my failings, I become terrified about how that is going to manifest itself. It's one of the reasons why I told Eric about my shortcomings early on. I said to him, "Listen, I believe that people have exactly 72 hours, or 3 dates, of getting to know each other while being completely honest, and after that you feel you have to protect yourself because of something you fear you will lose, because you become attached to the person, the job, the thing, whatever it is, so here it goes, here's my stuff..."

Several years ago I was in an interview process with a church, my first call actually, where I didn't believe I could be completely honest about my shortcomings because pastors don't have any, right? I was told by my bishop at the time not to disclose that my children were conceived by two different men. I mean, one was dead so I could deny him, it wasn't like he was going to come back and tell on me. I had to hide my debt because I was told after the fact, "how did you get through the candidacy process with all that debt." And so, when I failed at my first call, as some would perceive it, the controversy became a huge exposure of my shortcomings. I lost my first call, ended up in a mental institution with "adjustment disorder," and an indentation formed on my heart that I would never be accepted or loved. I felt betrayed and lost. So at times that becomes the story in my head. Those shortcomings became what I believed was my truth. These deceptions or tricks, as I like to call them, take me down a path of self-judgment and then I place those same judgments onto others.

Now lets translate that to all the others in the world that we place our judgment on. Because I am now rooted in the truth, that if God believes in me, clearly God believes in others. Some may say, "well I'm not as messed up as those people," but who are we to say that. We place levels on each other, just like we do with the idea of sin. But if God says, that we are blameless, sinless, that we are forgiven and love – who are we to say that the other is not because that is how God sees them. *ACIM* says, 'Hear of your brother what you would have me hear of you, for you would not want me to be deceived.[31]'

We all want good to be heard of us. But too often we take the time to point out someone's misfortune, misgivings, misunderstandings, and we miss all over the place. Because of this judgement of each other and misrepresentation, there is violence in our city streets, in the world, and sometimes even more so within ourselves. But what if we practiced forgiveness more frequently, more easily. If it moves us to accept others, and even ourselves, and maybe then we would stop seeing only the negative. No one person is better or more right than the other, no one.

So, I've discovered one thing in this journey,

---

[31] T-9.II.6:12

"love is not learned. Its meaning lies within itself. And learning ends when you have recognized all it is not. That is the interference; that is what needs to be undone. Love is not learned, because there NEVER was a time in which you knew it not. Learning is useless in the Presence of your Creator, Whose acknowledgment of you and yours of Him so far transcend all earning that everything you learned is meaningless, replaced forever by the knowledge of love and its one meaning.[32]"

ALL of our identity, OUR TRUE IDENTITY, is that we are love and that we are worthy of it and that should reignite our JOY.

---

[32] T-18.IX.12

A Time to Meditate

Marti Nikko and DJ Drez have a song that has become a personal mantra of mine. "I am love." That's all it says. "I am love" with different flavors and intonations in her voice. In this last meditation, maybe that is the meditation. Those are the words that you repeat to yourself, over and over again.

I. Am. Love.

WORKS CITED

Chodron, Pema. No Time to Loose: A Timely Guide to the Way of the Bodhisattva. Boston & London. Shambala Press. 2005

Lewis, C. S. The Four Loves (Harvest Book) (pp. 127-128). Houghton Mifflin Harcourt. Kindle Edition. 1971

Schucman, Helen. "A Course in Miracles." Mill Valley: Foundation for Inner Peace, 2007. Print.

Scovel-Shinn, Florence. "The Game of Life and How to Play it." 1928. Public Domain

Made in the USA
Middletown, DE
12 April 2018